STATION WAGON

A TRIBUTE TO AMERICA'S WORKAHOLIC ON WHEELS

Ron Kowalke

Published by

krause
publications

700 E. State Street • Iola, WI 54990-0001
Telephone: 715/445-2214

Please call or write for our free catalog.
Our toll-free number to place an order or obtain a free catalog is 800-258-0929
or please use our regular business telephone 715-445-2214
for editorial comment and further information.

Library of Congress Catalog Number: 97-80617
ISBN: 0-87341-567-1

Printed in the United States of America

Contents

Cover artist: Kevin Ulrich
Color section artist: Kevin Sauter
Pagination artist: Cheryl Mueller

**Arnie Beswick drag racing art
in color section courtesy of:**

Tim Frederick Studios
P.O. Box 4323
Timonium, MD 21094
(410)879-8831

Introduction

Through the years, the term station wagon has been applied to a variety of vehicle types in this country. Some of these vehicles, in reality, were either trucks or, very early on, almost bus-like. Later, some were compact cars with enhanced cargo bays. All of these station wagon "wannabes" were probably fine vehicles in their own right, but they did not possess any or all of the design features inherent in what we have historically come to accept as a "true" American station wagon.

For the scope of this book, the American station wagon—in its truest form—is defined as a long-wheelbase, rear-driven vehicle, most often having third-seat availability. That third seat is either forward- or rear-facing or, in some instances, dual center-facing. The Star Station Wagon of 1923-'24 is credited among many automotive historians as being the first "production" station wagon. This same body of historians generally recognizes the station wagon's demise as occurring in 1996. This is when production ended for the two rear-drive station wagon holdouts, the 1996 Buick Roadmaster Estate Wagon and Chevrolet Caprice Classic. This 1923 to 1996 time span represents 70 years of station wagon history (not including the three years when automobile production was halted due to World War II). Not bad for a vehicle that often, at best, received the faint praise of being utilitarian, spacious or a dependable "grocery-getter."

Robust production of American front-drive intermediate and compact station wagons continues today. These automobiles have no place in this book, however,

as they provide no link to the heritage of the "true" station wagon: The station wagon that, not so long ago, ruled the roads of suburbia; the station wagon that ably served as family transportation when the family unit was the backbone of our nation; and, the station wagon into which family members loaded vacation necessities and themselves and traveled out of suburbia seeking adventure and discovery on the highways of a burgeoning America. Sadly, along with the production of "true" station wagons, that adventurous, less time-managed way of life is also over. One purpose of this book, then, is to offer a glimpse of and rekindle the feeling of nostalgia for that bygone America where a modest home in suburbia, a station wagon in the garage of that home and children in the third-seat of that wagon were the American dream.

A revealing example of how much our way of life has changed is provided by longtime station wagon owner Ronald Anderson. The Newport Beach, Calif., resident recalls: "One clear memory [that] stands out after all these years involves [my 1966 Pontiac] Tempest. It suffered from the Phillips head screws holding the rear panel coverings working loose creating annoying little noises. The solution to this problem was to give our six-year-old son a Phillips head screwdriver and let him amuse himself in back tightening the many loose screws as we motored down the highway. A practice that will appall today's safety-oriented parents who grow their children in safety seats and seatbelts."

Don Chamberlain of Renton, Wash., writes: "This is my son, Robert Chamberlain test-driving a neighbor's new Murray Station Wagon with Jet Flow Drive. The picture was taken in San Diego in 1953 when Robert was just two years old. Forty-five years later, Robert is doing fine—but, unfortunately, no information as to the fate of the pedal car."

Station wagons, while forever revered by a small segment of old car hobbyists, seem to have struck the nostalgia chord among the more mainstream car collectors. Many wagons, especially the hardtops, are now as sought after as convertibles and coupes. As the car enthusiasts of the baby boomer generation look to acquire collector vehicles they cannot help recalling those family vacations of their youth, when Mom and Dad and brothers and sisters piled into the family station wagon and headed to Disneyland or the campgrounds or the beach. What better car to acquire, then, but a vintage station wagon that not only will transport a boomer age collector and his young family to the Magic Kingdom but also transport this collector back in time to cherished childhood memories.

Of the many interesting stories included in this book, one of the most important is the feature on the American Station Wagon Owners Association (ASWOA). If you are reading this book, you have at least a passing interest in station wagons. The members of ASWOA are passionate about station wagons. They work tirelessly to promote and preserve station wagons of all manufacturers. Their motto is: "Help Save the Whales"—both kind need saving, but in this case we are speaking of the type without the blowhole. To that end, if you are seriously considering undertaking an auto restoration project, how about reuniting a station wagon with its rightful platform, the highway. So many station wagons have been and are being destroyed in demolition derbies that their already low survival rate is further threatened. This does not bode well for future generations of car enthusiasts to own and enjoy the station wagons of the 1950s, 1960s and 1970s.

In addition to their popularity among the destruction derby set, station wagons have also made an impact on the sport of drag racing. The history of draggin' wagons is covered in-depth in this book by motorsports authority Phil Hall. His feature explodes the myth that station wagons have been "underachievers" in the motorsports arena with accounts of wagons that dominated the nation's dragstrips.

In keeping with the misconception of it being an underachiever at the strip, the station wagon also comes to mind last when thinking of high performance on the street. The fact is, many station wagons could be ordered from the factory with the "brute" big-block engine options offered by the manufacturers as well as three- and four-speed manual transmissions and rearend gear ratios that allowed for the wagon's utilitarian image to be left in a cloud of tire smoke! While hard to find, it is noteworthy that a few manufacturers hyped this mostly unheralded performance image of station wagons in their new car promotional materials.

Wagon Pioneers:
The Prewar Years

Station Wagon: Prewar Pioneers

Taking the approach of comic duo Abbott and Costello's famous routine "Who's on first?", we can ask "Whose was first?" for the claim of which automaker introduced the station wagon. Coming up with the answer is no less confusing than Bud Abbott enticing Lou Costello around the baseball diamond with "What's on second" and "I don't know's on third."

As early as 1901, there was the Woods Station Wagon, built by a Chicago-based maker of electric vehicles. It was similar in appearance to a motorized stagecoach and it was, indeed, a "station" wagon. It was meant to deliver passengers and luggage to the train station. This was also the case with many early automakers who contracted with outside craftsman—and in some cases, furniture companies—to produce wooden passenger compartments that could be mated to a maker's existing front sheet metal and chassis. These wood-and-metal-merger vehicles had several names, such as express or jitney (facing seats), but the common term for them was "depot hack." This name was derived from the fact that these vehicles mainly saw duty, again, delivering travelers and their luggage to the train depot.

Most of the early "hack-type" vehicles were open-front, open-sided and box-like in nature with a fixed top (also made of wood) with few passenger amenities. Some had roll-up canvas side curtains to ward off rain or snow. Many had jitney-type bench seats that folded up and out of the way to increase cargo space (these were, after all, work vehicles first and passenger conveyances second).

As with the aforementioned Woods electric and a few other makers' early examples, the term "station wagon" was used during the days of the depot hack, but it really gained prominence in 1923. This was the year that Star introduced what many—but not all—automotive historians consider the "first production station wagon." Star was part of ex-General Motors' executive William Crapo Durant's new New Jersey automotive empire. The Star Station Wagon was a typical open-sided, fixed-roof "hack" with three doors (two on the right, one on the left) and three forward-facing seats, the rear two of which could be removed for added cargo space. Cost of the Star Station Wagon was $610.

The number of craftsman/body builders creating the wood bodies for the early depot hacks and station wagons was large. Even Ford, by far the leading producer of early station wagons with its Model T depot hacks and, in 1928, Model A station wagons used outside body builders to assemble the passenger/cargo portions of its wagons. Henry Ford, always the innovator, decided that with the Model A all the wood pieces for the new station wagon would be produced at Ford's Iron Mountain, Mich., facility (many—but not all—wood pieces for the Model T depot hack were Ford-produced). Model A wagon parts were then shipped to the Murray Body Co. in Detroit for final assembly. Henry Ford owned vast reserves of forests (maple was the wood of choice) in Upper Michigan and it was lumber from these reserves that was used to produce the Model A station wagon's wooden pieces.

Ford continued to be the major producer of station wagons into the early 1930s, but the Great Depression of 1929 was taking its toll on wagon sales. Due to these diminished sales, Ford returned to using outside (read: less expensive) body builders to produce some of the wooden pieces for its station wagons. By 1933, only Ford, Dodge and Plymouth were offering station wagons as part of their total line of products. Each used outside craftsmen to assemble the wooden portions of these vehicles. In addition, as was the case for most station wagons of this era, they were classed and sold not as cars but as commercial vehicles (trucks).

By 1935, the station wagon was regaining its strength in numbers, due in part to the military ordering Dodge and Ford wagons for government use. In the following two years, several manufacturers not previously offering station wagons joined the sales race, including Hudson (Terraplane Station Wagon), Packard (Cantrell-bodied 120 model), Pontiac (Hercules body) and Studebaker (U.S. Body & Forging body). It was also in 1937 that Ford began assembling its station wagons at its Iron Mountain facility. This made Ford the first manufacturer to produce and assemble its station wagons, which were still classed as commercial vehicles. (Note: The 1923 Star Station Wagon was assembled off-site and shipped back to the factory for delivery whereas the 1937 Ford was produced at, assembled at and delivered from the factory. "Bud, who's on first?" ... "That's right, Lou!")

It was not until 1938 that a manufacturer offered a station wagon classed as a passenger automobile. That maker was Dodge, which, ironically, would not offer another station wagon after 1938 until the end of World War II (one prototype was built in 1939, but this Dodge wagon never reached mass production). By 1939, the wagon field was entering a multi-year expansion with both Chevrolet and Ford offering not one but two models of station wagons. Buick, Oldsmobile and Willys came aboard the wagon train the following year.

With war raging in other parts of the world in 1940, sales of station wagons in the United States were booming. Advances in the design of wagons allowed manufacturers to offer a much improved product. These advances included glass all-around becoming standard in most station wagons as well as the spare tire being moved inside the car (yes, wagons were now classed as passenger automobiles), this from its earlier sidemount and later tailgate-mounted external positions. Willys' aforementioned jump into the fray introduced the world to its Town and Country station wagon. This Town and Country model predated Chrysler's station wagon of the same name by a year. Crosley also introduced a wagon in 1940, a small, innovative two-door model that had steel doors with only the rear quarters and tailgate constructed of wood. The Crosley's "tailgate" was actually two doors that opened from the center in sedan delivery fashion.

If Crosley was the innovator of 1940, then the torch was passed to Chrysler in 1941. No warmed-over Willys here, Chrysler's Town & Country was a departure from what other station wagons had been up to this point. Chrysler even called its creation the Town & Country Car (partly for fanfare reasons to promote its new design, but speculation exists that it was also due to Willys' Town and Country Station Wagon released the year before—renamed American station wagon for 1941). What made Chrysler's Town & Country so revolutionary was that it resembled a four-door sedan; in fact, it used the all-steel roof panel of a seven-passenger sedan. Offered in both six- and nine-passenger versions, the T&C had no tailgate but rather a stationary rear window under which were a pair of center-opening, barrel-back doors. Chrysler eventually admitted this "Car" was a station wagon, and in its advertising called it the "smartest" wagon on the road. Almost lost in all the hype of Chrysler's deeds was that Mercury also offered a station wagon for the first time in 1940. It was based on a body shared with Ford.

After the Japanese invasion of Pearl Harbor in December of 1941, 1942 automobile production was short-lived. By February of that year, all automakers had ceased production of cars and trucks and converted their plants to assembling military weaponry. Each maker was able to produce some cars before the shutdown, but the majority of these vehicles were "confiscated" by the government to be rationed to those who made the "essential users" list, such as doctors, munitions plant workers and government officials. What few 1942 station wagons that were manufactured were favored for use as government fleet vehicles due to their multi-passenger capabilities.

As important as station wagons were in this time of war, their days, years and even decades of being both a desired mode of transportation as well as a shaper of American culture were yet to come.

1941 Station Wagon Production

Maker	Wagons Built	% of Total 1941 Cars Built
Willys	400	1.21
Chrysler Corp.*	3,707	11.20
Chevrolet*	4,790	14.47
Ford	16,766	50.64
Pontiac	1,714	5.18
Crosley	150	.45
Mercury	2,080	6.28
Oldsmobile	699	2.11
Buick	838	2.53
Packard	600	1.81
Hudson	179	.54

(*Ward's Automotive Yearbook 1949-'50*)

* Estimated

The Evolution of Ford's Station Wagon

Ronald Anderson of Newport Beach, Calif., writes: "My buddy and I owned this Model T Ford depot hack during our college days. The photo was taken in 1953 at the Festival of States Parade in St. Petersburg, Fla., during which the Model T blew steam to show it didn't like creeping along. In retrospect, stopping to change the flat tire on the rear might have provided the crowd some additional enjoyment. We later took the 'T' down to the frame and improved it considerably, including going back to wood-spoke wheels on the front."

Nineteen twenty-nine was the second year of Model A Ford production and the station wagon was again offered as a body style. Price of the wagon was $650, one of the most expensive models in Ford's lineup that year. Ford produced 4,954 wagons in 1929. This particular car is shown with the protective canvas side curtains in place, snapped to the outside of the wood framework.

A chauffeur-driven 1930 Model A Ford station wagon delivering passengers to the train station. Ford's wagon bodies continued to be made of maple from Upper Michigan forest reserves owned by Henry Ford. The bodies were assembled at either the Murray Body Co. in Detroit or by Baker-Rawling in Cleveland, Ohio. Designated Model #150-B, 3,510 station wagons were produced in 1930—a significant drop of over 1,400 units from the previous year, which was the beginning of the Great Depression.

By 1934, Ford station wagons were powered by V-8 engines although the four-cylinder was available—the final year until the 1971 Ford Pinto. Relatively unchanged from the 1933 wagon, Ford continued with "suicide" doors all around and bodies constructed of maple or birch. The V-8 wagon cost $660 and 2,905 were produced. The four-cylinder-powered wagon had only 95 units built, priced at $610 each.

The 1937 Ford station wagon was a landmark vehicle in several ways. Beginning in 1937, Ford became the first manufacturer to produce and assemble a wagon at its own factory, the company's Iron Mountain, Mich., facility. That year, headlights were incorporated into the front fenders for the first time. Both the front and rear doors opened at the B-pillar.

The spare tire on the 1937 Ford station wagon moved from the sidemount location of previous years to this tailgate-mounted location. Ford produced 9,304 wagons in 1937 priced at $755 for the Deluxe V-8 version.

The women were all smiling and the men all looked grumpy in this photo shoot of Ford's revolutionary 1937 station wagon. The wagon this year offered, as a $20 option, glass windows all around. The windshield and front doors utilized safety glass and the front door windows were of the crankdown variety. The rear door and quarter windows were sliding glass panes. Those gleaming whitewall tires were also optional equipment.

The 1939 Ford station wagon was offered in both Standard (above) and Deluxe (below) versions. Standard models (priced at $840 with 3,277 produced) carried the general styling of the 1938 Deluxe wagons including: a sharply veed grille with horizontal bars, headlights (shown with retrofitted round units) mounted inboard of the fenders and small side hood louvers. Deluxe models (priced at $920 with 6,155 produced) featured teardrop-shaped headlights blended into the leading edges of the front fenders, a grille set lower in the hood that carried vertical bars and simple chrome trim in place of hood louvers. Note that the Standard wagon has an upright exhaust extension associated with fording streams as well as a huge center push bar/bumper guard mounted on the front bumper. As the sign on the window reads, could this Ford have been outfitted for the abuse given a rental car?

Ford's Deluxe station wagon for 1940 featured new styling including: roofline revisions, horizontal grillework and chrome headlight trim rings with cast-in parking lights. All doors now opened from the rear. On this car, the bumper guards and whitewall tires were optional. Cost of the Deluxe wagon in 1940 was $950 with production totaling 8,730.

Prior to automobile production being stopped due to World War II, Ford was able to assemble 1,222 1942 station wagons in both Deluxe and Super Deluxe versions. Feb. 10, 1942, was Ford's final day of auto production until the war's end. This Super Deluxe model featured dark inset wood panels (light panels were the other choice). The bumper guards, whitewall tires and gravel shields were all optional equipment.

Other Oldies But "Woodies"

Studebaker

The door emblem on this 1933 Studebaker Series 56 station wagon reads "Veterans Administration," which makes this beautiful car a government fleet vehicle. This wagon was the creation of body builder J.T. Cantrell & Co. of Huntington, N.Y. Only a limited number of these wagons were built by Cantrell, on contract to Studebaker.

The 1939 Studebaker Commander Suburban station wagon had its body built by Peter McAvoy & Sons. Note the steep angle of the A-pillar. All doors opened at the B-pillar. Glass all-around was standard on this wagon.

Terraplane

An artist's rendering of the 1936 Terraplane Series 62 station wagon. This was the first year a station wagon was offered by Hudson-Terraplane. The car was priced at $750 and featured Bendix hydraulic brakes on all four wheels as well as 16-inch wheels.

Buick

In 1937, a station wagon was years away from being a Buick offering—coming on-line in 1940 as the Super Estate Wagon. This wood-bodied wagon, based on a 1937 Buick Special, is a custom-built car. All door and quarter windows have glass and a forward-facing third seat is visible. If the car would have been offered for sale in 1937, those whitewall tires would have been optional equipment.

Willys

An artist's rendering of the 1940 Deluxe station wagon, the first wagon offered by Willys. While the car appears to be rather long in the drawing it actually rode on a small 102-inch wheelbase. Willys named this car the Town and Country, which was the name of Chrysler's wagon the very next year. Willys only produced 21,418 cars in 1940 among five models, so it can be assumed that wagon production was minuscule at best. The car was powered by a four-cylinder engine.

Pontiac

Hercules was the body builder for this 1938 Pontiac station wagon made of white ash-framing and mahogany panels. Price of the six-cylinder-powered car was $1,110 and glass was featured all-around. Two combinations of colors were available for this wagon: maroon with red striping or brown with cream striping. Even in its second year of availability, Pontiac still had not assigned a model number to its station wagon, which was simply referred to as STA WAG in company literature.

Hercules was again the body builder in 1942 for Pontiac's station wagon. That year, the wagon was offered in both base Streamliner (three seats) and Chieftain (two seats) versions. The Streamliner was available with either a six-cylinder or straight-eight engine, was priced at $1,265 or $1,290, respectively, and featured rubber mats and leather-composition interior fabric. This wagon was powered by the straight-eight and had a 16-gallon gas tank. Pontiac halted production of its automobiles on Feb. 10, 1942, due to World War II.

Front and rear views of this 1941 Pontiac Deluxe Custom Torpedo station wagon show the beautiful wood work of the Hercules Body Co. of Evansville, Ind. Pontiac also used Ionia wood bodies in 1941 and these had a more rounded appearance at the rear compared to the Hercules-bodied wagons. This car had white ash framing filled in with mahogany panels. The Deluxe wagon (a standard version was also offered with a six-cylinder engine) featured a straight-eight engine, and the interior had chrome-plated seat frames and leather seat cushions. The back seat and cargo areas were both carpeted. The fender-mounted antenna signifies this Deluxe wagon had a radio. Price of the standard wagon was $1,200 while the Deluxe package added $50 to the cost of the car. The bumper wing tips, whitewall tires and wheel trim rings were all optional equipment.

18

Oldsmobile

Oldsmobile factory records for 1935 do not record any station wagons being built. This photograph proves at least one, and, based on speculation, as many as "a handful" were assembled, with the body builder most likely being U.S. Body & Forging Co. of Tell City, Ind. The six-cylinder-powered car featured "suicide" front doors. Mounting hasps for side curtains are visible on the rear framework signifying crankdown windows were available only in the front doors.

The guy getting ready to load luggage into this 1940 Oldsmobile station wagon was all smiles until he opened the tailgate and discovered the third seat had to be removed to make cargo space available! This wagon was assembled by Hercules and featured white ash framing and birch finish panels. The car was offered as a Series 60 Olds at a price of $1,042. Total production was 633. The wagon's spare tire was mounted on the tailgate, and each car came with a special tool kit mounted under the front seat.

Hudson

In 1941, Hudson offered a station wagon in both its Super Six series (priced at $1,297) and Commodore Eight series (priced at $1,383). The body builder for each was J.T. Cantrell & Co. of Huntington, N.Y. Both the wagon's front and rear doors had crankdown glass. Sliding glass made up the quarter windows. The spare tire was mounted on the tailgate. This is the Super Six version with Hockanum Tweed interior. The Commodore Eight's interior fabric was Hockanum Twill Cord.

Packard

The dark wood framing suggests a Cantrell body, but as of 1940, Packard station wagon bodies were constructed by Hercules Body Co. This Junior Packard wagon was the new-for-1940 110 model. It featured crankdown windows in the doors and sliding quarter windows. The spare tire was located inside the cargo area. Price of the six-cylinder-powered car was $1,200.

One year later, the 1941 Packard 110 station wagon had undergone several major styling changes as well as being offered in standard (priced at $1,251) and Deluxe (priced at $1,326) versions. This is the Deluxe version, powered by a six-cylinder engine. Ash framing and mahogany panels made up the body by Hercules.

Chrysler

In March of 1941, Chrysler introduced its Town & Country Car (station wagon) as part of its Royal Six series. The T&C wagon was offered in two versions: a six-passenger model (priced at $1,412) and this nine-passenger model (priced at $1,492). The Chrysler's revolutionary design included an all-steel roof panel and a rounded/sloping rear treatment that was a departure from other station wagons of the time. The body was also steel covered with white ash framing and mahogany veneer panels. All wood products were supplied by Chrysler subsidiary Pekin Wood Products Co. of Helena, Ark. Production totals were 200 for the six-passenger T&C and 796 for the nine-passenger T&C.

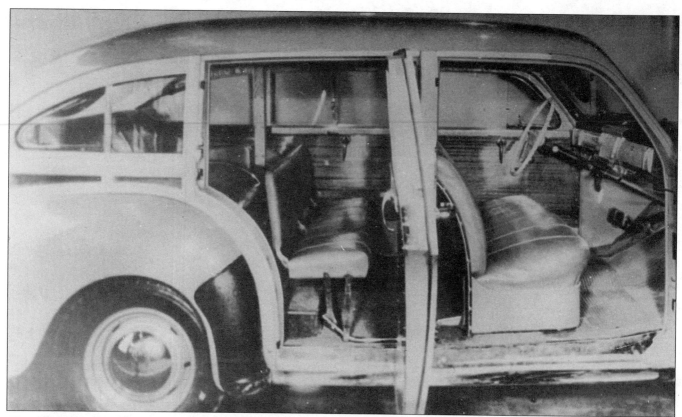

The interior of the T&C wagon utilized the same white ash and mahogany as was used on the exterior surfaces. This nine-passenger model featured the center auxiliary seat in place, which, when not in use, could be folded flush against the front seat.

The Town & Country wagon featured a "barrel-back" design instead of a tailgate, with two rear doors that opened from the center. Due to the rear window being stationary, the Chrysler's cargo space was more trunk-like than wagon-like. The front doors and quarter windows featured vent "wing" windows. The rear doors used sliding glass.

Apart from revised frontal styling and door bottoms that "kicked out" to conceal runningboards, the 1942 Chrysler Town & Country station wagon was not much changed from its previous introductory year. It was upgraded into the Windsor Six series. The front view (above) has the car loaded with optional equipment including roof rack, mirror hubcaps, whitewall wheel discs and spotlight. The rear view (below) is the standard version. All glass was safety laminated. This nine-passenger version was priced at $1,685 and 849 were produced prior to Chrysler halting its automobile production in January 1942 due to World War II. The six-passenger T&C was also offered and was priced at $1,595. Only 150 were built.

Wagon Conversions Aid the War Effort

Monart Motors Co. of Milwaukee, Wis., provided a vital service to America during World War II. No, the company didn't build tanks, or fighter planes or artillery shells. What Monart did build were 9-to-12-passenger station wagon conversions based on either Mercury coupes or sedans.

The reason for the conversions was simple—given the rationing of the time. A station wagon can transport many more people than a coupe or sedan. With automobile production stopped in February of 1942, all "new" cars (mainly 1941 and 1942 models) were basically mothballed and became the property of the U.S. Government. These cars were distributed only to "essential users" such as doctors, munitions plant workers, Civil Defense workers and government officials.

Within a short time, this rationed supply of automobiles became low, and, in fact, the supply of station wagons was exhausted. Monart, a Mercury dealer prior to the war, created a program to offset this shortage. This program consisted of converting "mothballed" Mercury coupes (which held the fewest passengers) and, if needed, sedans, into two- and four-door station wagons, respectively, with seating arrangements capable of accommodating as many as a dozen passengers.

Aside from helping to bolster passenger capacity in cars used by civilians and the government in a time of rationing, the Monart conversions also aided the war effort in another way. How is explained in the company's brochure, titled *Conservation in the War Effort*: "These conversions have been executed entirely of wood and non-strategic materials throughout with the exception of bolts, screws, and bracings. The conversion also releases, for complete salvage, several hundred pounds of steel in unused body parts."

Noted industrial designer and engineer Brooks Stevens was hired by Monart Motors Co. to help create the conversions, called Monart Mercury Carry-All Station Wagons. While the cost of a conversion Carry-All was not revealed in Monart's brochure, adding all the individual prices listed together puts the total at approximately $1,950 (including the $1,150 cost of the original Mercury coupe). The number of conversion Mercury station wagons created by Monart Motors Co. and Brooks Stevens is unknown. No Carry-All conversion is known to exist today to study one of these fascinating "war wagons."

Monart Motors Co. of Milwaukee, Wis., produced this patriotic-looking brochure titled *Conservation in the War Effort* to promote its Monart Mercury Carry-All Station Wagon conversion, designed by Brooks Stevens. (Photo courtesy of Brooks Stevens Collection)

An August 1942 design rendering by Brooks Stevens of a Monart Mercury Carry-All Station Wagon conversion. (Photo courtesy of Brooks Stevens Collection)

A stock Mercury sedan at left and the four-door Carry-All Station Wagon conversion it became at right at Monart Motors Co. (Photo courtesy of Brooks Stevens Collection)

The nine-passenger Carry-All with sliding-glass quarter windows. (Photo courtesy of Brooks Stevens Collection)

A two-door Monart Mercury Carry-All Station Wagon conversion with lengthwise seating for up to 10 passengers. (Photo courtesy of Brooks Stevens Collection)

A Mercury two-door coupe undergoing conversion to a two-door Carry-All Station Wagon—most likely for ambulance duty. (Photo courtesy of Brooks Stevens Collection)

Wagon Masters:
The Postwar Years

Masters of the Suburban Universe

By the end of World War II, the United States was, as a nation, weary from grieving for war casualties and dealing with wartime shortages and the ensuing hardships caused by rationing. While it would be a long time before this war-induced anguish would pass completely, the immediate postwar years were also a time for optimism. More importantly, these were rebuilding years; the piecing back together of shattered lives, broken families, interrupted careers and the long-dormant transportation network. Americans, no longer grounded by rationing, returned to being consumers. These consumers wanted cars. The war had temporarily stolen their freedom, and what better way to experience the exhilaration of regained freedom than cruising unencumbered in a new automobile.

The postwar demand for cars exceeded the available supply. Harried manufacturers had to re-convert assembly plants from war materiel production back to automobile manufacturing. For the first few years after the war, most "new" automobiles were merely warmed-over 1942 models cranked out to meet this heavy consumer demand. The wood-bodied station wagons offered by manufacturers before the war—most of which were assembled by off-site body builders under contract to the automakers—quickly gave way to the more practical all-steel-bodied wagons. The "woodie" look would continue, though, but evolved into an imitation wood trim that was now decorative rather than structural. By 1952, station wagons were offered by most—but not all—of the manufacturers and they sold in moderate numbers. That all changed in the mid-1950s—the beginning of the station wagon boom years—when "tailgate mania" swept the nation.

Station Wagon Sales—1951 to 1963

Model Year	Wagons Built	Total U.S. Cars Built	% Wagons
1951	174,500	5,312,000	3.3
1952	168,500	4,306,000	3.9
1953	303,000	6,131,500	4.9
1954	310,000	4,800,000	6.5
1955	580,000	7,045,500	8.2
1956	707,200	6,288,700	11.3
1957	843,500	6,212,000	13.6
1958	647,000	4,260,000	15.2
1959	937,000	5,563,000	16.9
1960	923,700	6,011,000	15.4
1961	866,800	5,408,600	16.0
1962	924,900	6,686,000	13.8
1963	963,500	7,340,000	13.1

(Ward's Automotive Yearbook - 1964)

In the years 1951 to 1954 and then again in 1954 to 1957, station wagons approximately doubled their share of total U.S. automobile production. The variety of station wagon models offered by each manufacturer at that time was also impressive. In addition to the wagon's skyrocketing sales, another revolution was taking place. The wagon was leaving behind its utilitarian roots and evolving into a style leader. The hardtop station wagon, especially, was a beautiful design, and most manufacturers embraced the chance to offer a top-of-the-line wagon that was both functional and fancy.

Along with hardtop styling, the station wagon also embraced the auto industry's late-1950s affinity for chrome and tailfins. The Buick, Rambler and Dodge station wagons of this period are all shining and pointed examples of this design trend. As with the hardtop models from this time, the other highly sought after station wagons by modern car collectors are the Chevrolet Nomad and Pontiac Safari, both originating as two-door "sport" wagons in 1955. While innovative in design, the presumed "big" sales of Nomad/Safari wagons never materialized. After the quick demise of the two-door versions, both the Nomad and Safari names were carried over to four-door station wagon models. The Safari name would continue to identify Pontiac station wagons into the 1990s.

Also of note in this time of manufacturers upgrading their station wagons was Studebaker's 1957 attempt at going in the other direction. That maker's four model Champion series of wagons included the Scotsman, a plain, economy two-door wagon devoid of all chrome except its bumpers. Companion two- and four-door sedans were also offered in the Scotsman line. In its initial offering in 1957, the Scotsman wagon found 3,400 buyers. In its second—and last—year, 1958 sales of the virtually unchanged Scotsman wagon more than doubled to 7,680. In comparison to other Studebaker station wagon sales for those two years, the Scotsman's sell-through was outstanding. However, having the exclusive market for an economy station wagon that was both inexpensive to build and a decent seller just was not enough to continue production of the radical Studebaker.

In the annals of station wagon history, 1960 was recorded as the year of both big and small introductions. The "big" introduction was the first-time offering of the non-fleet Checker Superba station wagon. The "small" introduction was the almost across-the-board first-time offering of compact station wagons by two of the "Big Three" makers. Ford introduced its Falcon wagon (counterpart Mercury, as well, offered a similar Comet wagon). The Falcon station wagon measured 189 inches long with a wheelbase of 109.5 inches. This compared to the top-line Ford Country Squire wagon's measurements of 213.7 inches and 119 inches, respectively. Over at Chrysler Corp., Plymouth unveiled the Valiant wagon. It, too, was dwarfed by its big brother Belvedere and Fury wagons.

The remaining "Big Three" player, Chevrolet, brought its compact Corvair Lakewood station wagon on line in 1961. This rear-engine Chevy was joined that year by compact wagons (all front-engine models based on the same body shell) from GM counterparts Buick, Oldsmobile and Pontiac. All this "downsizing" was carried out voluntarily to compete with the smaller offerings of foreign manufacturers that were attracting first-time and young-parent car buyers looking for economical transportation. No one at the time could foresee the similar, but forced, station wagon "downsizing" that would occur approximately one decade later due to the energy crisis and, again, competition from abroad. This early-1970s smaller-for-better-mpg movement would, in part, be responsible for the eventual demise of the long-wheelbase, rear-driven station wagon some 20 years later.

The next logical progression of new model station wagon offerings occurred in 1962. That year, intermediate-size wagons were introduced by Chevrolet (Chevy II) and Ford (Fairlane). These mid-size wagons offered car buyers a step up from the compacts. In 1963, for the first time since Willys introduced its two-door Jeep station wagon in 1946—regarded as the auto industry's "only true station wagon" (not a derivative of a sedan)—a four-door Jeep wagon was offered. (A few four-door Jeeps were produced prior to 1963 for railroad track maintenance duties, but these were never meant for public sale.) Control of the Jeep also passed from Willys to Kaiser Corp. in 1963.

Just as the Jeep was a Brooks Stevens' design, his talents were responsible for another innovative station wagon, the 1963 Studebaker Lark Daytona Wagonaire. This unique wagon offered a forward-sliding rear roof panel and a tailgate-attached one-rung step that folded into the gate. With the roof panel slid forward, the Wagonaire could haul tall objects upright, not unlike cargo carried in the bed of a pickup truck.

During the early-1960s, innovations introduced on station wagons was becoming a game of "one-upsmanship" among the manufacturers. In 1964, General Motors' Oldsmobile and Buick Divisions introduced the Vista Cruiser and Sportwagon station wagons, respectively. These two wagons shared the same body shell, which featured a domed roof containing tinted glass panels above the rear passenger compartment (called the "Skyroof" on Buicks). Over the following two years, Ford got everyone's attention with both its revolutionary dual center facing rear (third) seats and its "Magic Doorgate." This doorgate was the pioneering variable-opening (pulls down or swings open) gate that soon became the industry norm.

Closing out the 1960s, automakers relied less on innovation and more on product refinement to sell their wagons. Wood appliqué became trendy and was used by all the manufacturers to lend an upscale "image" to a particular model. Creature comforts such as state-of-the-art sound systems and "sport" themed interior options including bucket seats, leather-grained steering wheel, armrests and headrests all found their way into the station wagons of one manufacturer or another.

Use of wood appliqué on station wagons continued unabated into the 1970s, with Ford actually giving this treatment the name Squire Package. In 1970, AMC introduced the Sportabout wagon, which was based on the Hornet chassis. The Sportabout featured the pioneering hatchback rather than a tailgate. As for the other manu-facturers' wagons, some form of the dual-action doorgate was now the rule rather than the exception. Buick's "Skyroof" was no longer offered in 1970. Oldsmobile's similar domed roof treatment, as well as the Vista Cruiser station wagon on which it was offered, would be discontinued the following year.

Offsetting the loss of the Vista Cruiser in 1971, Oldsmobile introduced the Custom Cruiser station wagon. Part of the novelty of this large, 127-inch wheelbase wagon was that it featured General Motors' new "Clam Shell" tailgate. As the name implied, this gate separated at the meeting point of glass and metal with the rear window sliding up into the roof and the tailgate sliding down under the floor. Due, in part, to the popularity of AMC's Sportabout introduced the year before, Chevrolet unveiled its Vega line of small cars. This series included the Vega 2300 two-door Kammback Wagon, which also featured a hatchback as well as bucket seats and seating for five.

Never one to be left behind, in 1972, Ford introduced its Pinto line of small cars. The Pinto two-door station wagon could be ordered with the Squire Package to create the upscale look in a very downsized automobile. With mass acceptance of both the Vega and Pinto wagons, as well as the imported small wagons being offered by several other makers, the extinction of the behemoth station wagon was fast approaching.

In 1974, the auto industry as a whole was blindsided by the energy crisis. Whether this "crisis" was real or contrived remains a point of debate even today. Controversial or not, it was the catalyst for sweeping change in American automobile production. From that point on, Detroit put its energy into building cars that were leaner and cleaner (lower emissions). The larger station wagons that were offered before the fuel shortage and remained in production after were now powered by smaller or emasculated engines in an effort to achieve better gas mileage.

The Dodge Aspen and Plymouth Volare wagons, both introduced in 1976, were representative of post-energy crisis Detroit products. Both Chrysler Corp. six-passenger wagons were offered in both base and deluxe (read: wood appliqué) versions. Each came standard with six-cylinder power, but had two "reasonable" V-8 engine options. This tiered approach to selling automobiles allowed buyers to select not only their station wagon's model and trim level, but also their desired mpg based on engine selection.

By the mid-1980s, many models of station wagons that were formerly large enough to cast major shadows were either discontinued or became mere shadows of their former selves. With 1987's departure of AMC—swallowed whole by Chrysler—production of the long-running, innovative four-wheel-drive Eagle station wagon was discontinued. The larger station wagons could not survive in this new age of lightweight aluminum- and plastic-component cars that by government mandate were expected to achieve ever higher mpg numbers. The manufacturers' exodus away from rear-wheel-drive to adopt front-wheel-drive allowed for only a handful of rear-driven station wagons to remain in production into the 1990s. The Buick Roadmaster, Chevrolet Caprice Classic, Ford LTD Crown Victoria, Mercury Grand Marquis Colony Park and Oldsmobile Custom Cruiser were these lone survivors. They were produced to satisfy the lingering demand of "traditionalist" buyers who wanted only the spacious, rear-drive wagons they had been buying and driving for years. By 1993, three of the aforementioned five makers, Ford, Mercury and Oldsmobile, had stopped producing rear-drive wagons.

Closing out of the 1980s, the drawingboards in Detroit were filled with sketches of a new, revolutionary type of family transport. Called the minivan, it quickly became the automotive version of utilitarian utopia, offering ample room for an entire family, plush interiors and the all-important cupholder for every passenger. The Buick Roadmaster and Chevrolet Caprice Classic station wagons remained in production until 1996. Their demise marked the end of seven-plus decades of domestic, rear-drive, long-wheelbase station wagon production. The workhorse wagon that had spent those many decades transporting families in and out of suburbia and over the scenic highways of America had now been left behind on the road of progress.

Hardtop Wagons: Hauling Cargo in Style

Utilitarian. Boxy. Family car. These are the names often heard when a station wagon is described. Well, how about stylish, luxurious or just downright eye-catching? What? A station wagon that's pretty?

Station wagons experienced enormous gains in both popularity and sales during the 1950s. The reason for these gains was due, in part, to manufacturers offering wagons with design features that mimicked the makers' hot-selling sport coupes and sedans. From this mimicry sprang the hardtop station wagon—working hauler by day and luxury cruiser by night.

The hardtop station wagons offered by American Motors/Rambler, Chrysler, Ford and General Motors from the mid-1950s to mid-1960s represented those manufacturers' top-of-the-line products. Building a station wagon was already an expensive proposition when compared to producing a sedan or even a convertible. Offering a hardtop version of the wagon only added cost to this bottom line.

Most buyers of hardtop station wagons sought luxury, ordering option-laden vehicles that surrounded their drivers in creature comforts. Conventional wagons were available at much less cost, so the "typical" buyer of a hardtop wagon usually took the spare-no-expense approach into the dealership.

As with most station wagons, the survival rate of these unique and stylish hardtop versions is not great. While the word "rare" is often overused in the old car hobby, these wagons were never built in great numbers to begin with so the math is pretty simple. Because most hardtop station wagons were well-appointed from the factory, their desirability as collector cars is high—both for this luxury and for their good looks.

The 1956 Nash Rambler Custom Cross Country hardtop station wagon was credited with being the originator of this style, which was adopted by other manufacturers the following year. The "paneling" was simulated wood. The downslope of the wagon's roof was created by an additional panel being welded on to lengthen a sedan roof. This grafting process was done as a money saving measure.

In 1957, the Nash Rambler Custom Cross Country hardtop station wagon retained the simulated wood trim and downsloping rear roof. The central pillar carried the badge that signified the car was powered by a V-8 engine. This car cost $2,715, but even at that low price only 182 were produced.

The operation of the two-piece tailgate is evident in this shot of a 1957 Oldsmobile 88 Fiesta hardtop station wagon loaded for a camping trip. This "pillarless" styling was new for General Motors' station wagons that year. Cost of a 88 Fiesta was $3,017 and 5,767 were built.

Hardtop styling was also new to Mercury station wagons in 1957. There were three different models offered that year and this Voyager was the mid-level wagon, positioned between the top-line Colony Park and base Commuter. The eight-passenger Voyager was priced at $3,403 and 3,716 were built.

The 1958 Buick Century hardtop station wagon was called the Caballero Estate Wagon. Caballero was Spanish for knight or horseman, although no suit of armor ever had this much chrome. This was Buick's top-line wagon for 1958, and could be purchased for $3,831. Total production was 4,456.

Similar in appearance to Buick's Caballero, the 1958 Oldsmobile Super 88 Fiesta hardtop station wagon was also the top-line model for that automaker. Production totaled 5,175, which was quite a drop from the year before (3,806 fewer). The car's price was $3,623 (up $400 from the year previous).

Ford Motor Co. was alone in featuring simulated wood on the sides of its cars in 1958. This six-passenger Mercury Colony Park hardtop station wagon was again the top-line offering from Mercury, which was reflected in its price of $3,775. Production totaled 4,474.

The 1959 Rambler Ambassador Custom Country Club hardtop station wagon was no different from most other cars of the period when it came to having "tall tails" to sell. While not quite up to the stature of a 1959 Cadillac's fins, this Ambassador's tailfins were impressive. The roof rack on top of the sloping rear panel was still part of the design of this Rambler wagon, priced at $3,026. An optional reclining front seat added $25.50 to the cost. A total of 4,341 were built.

In 1960, Dodge's top-line station wagon was the Polara series. The Polara wagon featured hardtop styling while the other three Dodge wagon series offered that year did not. In addition to being Dodge's most expensive wagon at $3,621, the Polara was also Dodge's heaviest at 4,220 pounds (both figures for the nine-passenger version). Note the "assist" handles attached to the car's D-pillars to aid entry and exit over the laydown tailgate.

Both the six- and nine-passenger versions of the 1961 Chrysler New Yorker hardtop station wagon had the distinction of being the highest-priced American wagons on the market. Priced at $4,764 and $4,871, respectively, production numbers on these top-line Chryslers were extremely low: 676 and 760, respectively. Chrysler cars were among the few in 1961 still sporting prominent tailfins.

Remaining the highest-priced American station wagon on the market, the 1963 Chrysler New Yorker wagon also continued to offer a hardtop model after other manufacturers abandoned this styling cue. Available in both six- and nine-passenger capacities, prices and production totals were, respectively: $3,478 and $3,586 and 3,618 and 2,948. In 1963, Chrysler introduced the extended warranty with "America's first five-year or 50,000-mile automobile warranty" on all of its passenger cars.

Beautifully illustrated in factory sales literature, this six-passenger 1963 Dodge Custom 880 station wagon was one of the final wagons to offer hardtop styling (1964 Chrysler and Dodge wagons would be the last designed as hardtops). In the literature, Dodge promoted its Custom 880 stating: "This automobile handles and rides with a stately beauty all its own. To drive it is a rewarding experience. ...the most elegant automobile ever fashioned by Dodge." This six-passenger Custom 880 sold for $3,292 and was a rewarding experience for 1,647 buyers while the nine-passenger version cost $3,407 and garnered 1,365 sales.

Cargo Space Race

Jeep

While this 1946 Willys Jeep two-door station wagon appeared "woodie-like," it was actually an all-steel body made to simulate the popular wood-bodied wagons of the immediate postwar period. The Jeep wagon was designed by Brooks Stevens. It was a merging of the famed Willys military vehicle's frontal styling and the Stevens' designed passenger compartment. Note the spare tire mounted inside the rear compartment. The single seats in the rear were removable to gain additional cargo space.

Apart from the simulated caning at the beltline, the 1949 Willys Jeep two-door station wagon was pretty much unchanged from previous years. Other than minor styling changes from year to year, this same basic Jeep wagon would remain in production through 1965. The Jeep wagon featured a two-piece tailgate.

In 1950, Willys offered two series of Jeeps. The first series was nothing more than carried-over 1949 models. The second series, including this two-door station wagon, was available after April 16, 1950. Grilles of the second series Jeeps featured a veed shape with five chrome horizontal bars attached. The "woodie" look was still in use, but not for long.

Packard

Packard's first postwar station wagon was this 1948 Station Sedan. The 22nd Series Standard Packard featured northern birch wood body paneling that was structural only in the tailgate section. Price was $3,350.

Not since the 1950 Station Sedan had Packard offered a station wagon until this 1957 Clipper Country Sedan. This Packard was a badge-engineered automobile built off a Studebaker President chassis. The roof rack on this six-passenger wagon was a $60 option. Both the front and rear door windows contained vent "wings." The Clipper's tailgate was a two-piece unit. The Country Sedan was priced at $3,384 and only 869 were built.

The 1958 Packard station wagon was the "no name" wagon. Packard was but a shadow of its former self by this time and in July of 1958 would cease production forever. This wagon was essentially a warmed-over Clipper from the year before. A "Rideaway" third seat was optional for $101.68. The car's base price remained unchanged at $3,384, and only a paltry 159 were produced.

Cadillac

Cadillac never offered a station wagon in its line of products, but the marque's popularity spawned several aftermarket versions of wagons built in its image. This 1951 "Cadillac" station wagon was a product of Coachcraft of California. The wagon was based on a Series 62 chassis, and featured a pow-er-operated rear window that retracted into the tailgate.

Another aftermarket manufacturer of "Cadillac" station wagons was Hess and Eisenhardt of Ohio. That company also utilized the Series 62 chassis to create this 1956 wagon, reportedly one of only 12 produced that year. This wagon was powered by the 305-hp Eldorado V-8 engine, and had an all-leather interior.

Nash

A 1952 Nash Rambler Greenbrier two-door station wagon posed on a lush fairway of a country club. The Greenbrier was Nash's top-line wagon and featured two-tone paint and richer trim. A total of 4,425 Greenbriers were produced in 1952.

Termed a "compact," this 100-inch wheelbase 1953 Nash Rambler Custom two-door station wagon included the "Weather-Eye" conditioned air system and a radio as standard equipment. It was priced at $2,119 and 10,598 were produced. The center windows had sliding glass.

Rambler

The 1956 Rambler Custom Cross Country station wagon had 80 cubic feet of cargo space. The roof rack was standard equipment. Price of the six-passenger wagon was $2,326.

Only minor trim changes distinguished the 1957 Rambler Custom Cross Country station wagon from its predecessor. Optional equipment for this wagon included "airliner" reclining seats with twin-bed combination. This wagon was based on single-unit body construction, and was offered in 15 colors including 12 two-tone and 5 three-tone combinations.

Two views of the 1959 Rambler American Super two-door station wagon. Wheelbase was 100 inches. Cargo space was 52 cubic feet. This wagon was priced at $2,145 and 17,383 were produced. The center windows used sliding glass. Two-tone paint combinations were a $17.95 option.

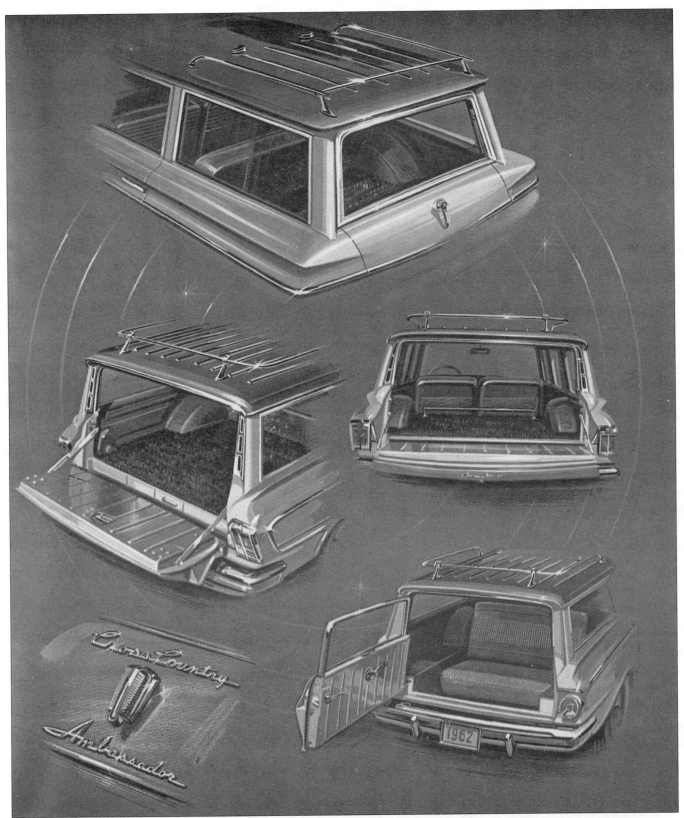

Its factory literature reads: "1962 Rambler Station Wagons are built for style, stamina and <u>living</u> room!" There were three series of Rambler wagons in 1962: Classic, Ambassador and American. They were offered in two-door, four-door and five-door configurations with two-seats or three-seats available. The literature also reads: "If lively station wagon living is for you, see your Rambler dealer ... your station wagon headquarters."

When both vehicles were new in 1962, the child's racer probably cost one-fifth of the $2,640 price of the 1962 Rambler Classic 400 station wagon. In today's automobilia marketplace, that mini-racer would bring twice the value of the wagon in excellent condition. The Rambler aluminum six-cylinder engine powered this 400 wagon, which featured 80 cubic feet of cargo space. Production totaled 21,281.

Two rear views of the 1965 Rambler Classic 770 Cross Country station wagon. The 770 was the top trim level wagon of the three-model (also 550 and 660) Classic series. It featured seating for six and the roof rack was standard equipment. The vent windows in the back doors were non-functional. Price of the 770 wagon was $2,727 and 15,623 were built.

Two views of the 1965 Rambler Ambassador 990 Cross Country station wagon. The 990 was the top trim level wagon of the two-model (also 880) Ambassador series. Ramblers in 1965 were marketed under the slogan "The Sensible Spectaculars." Price of the 990 wagon was $2,970. A total of 8,701 were produced.

Now identified as an American Motors product, the 1967 AMC Rambler Rebel 770 Cross Country station wagon offered a 5-year/50,000-mile warranty on its engine and drivetrain. Totally redesigned from its predecessor Classic 770 wagon, the Rebel 770 rode on a 114-inch wheelbase. Simulated woodgrain trim was a $100 option. A third seat for nine-passenger capacity was also optional for $112. The Rebel 770 wagon was priced at $2,710 and 18,240 were produced.

The Westerner, which featured a ranch theme, was one of three special 1967 Rambler Rebel station wagons designed by AMC for spring and summer sale in the Midwest and Southwest. The wagon's frost white body was highlighted by simulated natural tan leather grain panels that ran the full length of the sides. Stallion brown vinyl (with an appearance similar to rich tooled leather) carried out the Western look inside. Only 500 of the Westerners were built while 400 of the Rebel Briarcliff were built and sold in the eastern U.S. and 600 of the Rebel Mariner were produced and sold in coastal areas of the United States.

The 1968 AMC Rambler Rebel 770 station wagon offered buyers a choice of a drop tailgate or side-hinged tailgate. The rooftop travel rack was standard equipment as was the simulated wood treatment. This car carried the badge signifying it had the optional 290-cid V-8. The Rebel 770 wagon was priced at $2,854 and 11,375 were produced.

AMC's top-line station wagon for 1968 was the Rambler Ambassador DPL priced at $3,207 (10,690 were built). This could be considered an action shot with the wagon pulling a Century travel trailer. This DPL wagon was fitted with the optional front sway bar and heavy-duty springs and shocks to pull a behemoth such as the Century.

A late release (spring) for the 1971 model year was this AMC Hornet Sportabout station wagon with D/L package. This package included imitation woodgrain side panels, roof rack with integral air deflector, custom wheelcovers, individual reclining seats, imitation woodgrain instrument cluster trim and D/L graphics for the exterior.

The 1971 AMC Matador station wagon featured the "Dual-Swing" tailgate. This Matador was loaded with optional equipment including: 360-cid V-8 ($97), imitation woodgrain side panels ($117), roof rack ($58) and rear air deflector ($22). Base price of the Matador wagon was $3,493 and 10,740 were produced.

The top-line station wagon for AMC in 1971 was the Ambassador Brougham with the imitation woodgrain side panels. Standard equipment on this wagon included air conditioning, roof rack and individually adjustable reclining seats. This Ambassador had the optional ($118) third, rear-facing seat and power tailgate. Base price of the Ambassador Brougham wagon was $4,430 and 5,479 were built.

This 1975 AMC Matador station wagon sported the $145 Brougham option package as well as the $121 third, rear-facing seat option. With the demise of the Ambassador line of cars after 1974, the Matador became AMC's top-line station wagon. With V-8 power, this wagon was base priced at $3,943 and 8,117 were built while with the six-cylinder engine the base price was $3,844 and 1,575 were built.

The 1972 AMC Hornet line offered a designer Sportabout station wagon created by Italian fashion giant Dr. Aldo Gucci. The "Gucci" Sportabout's interior featured boldly striped green, red and buff vinyl seats and door panels matched to a color-keyed headliner. The wagon was offered in four colors: Snow white, Hunter green, Grasshopper green and Yucca tan. Individually adjustable reclining front seats were standard equipment while the sun roof pictured was optional. A total of 2,583 were produced.

AMC introduced its four-wheel-drive Eagle station wagon in 1980, and also offered a "tamer" rear-drive wagon of similar design called the Concord. The Concord wagon was offered in three levels of trim: base, D/L and Limited. This 1980 Concord Limited wagon featured woodgrain appliqué and optional roof rack ($93) and wire wheel covers ($15). Price of the Concord Limited was $5,876 with four-cylinder engine and $6,005 with six-cylinder powerplant.

Checker

One of the unique features of the 1960 Checker Superba Special station wagon was the dash panel control button used to the lower the rear seat. The price of this Superba Special wagon was $3,004 and production was limited as this was the first year Checkers were sold in the private car market.

How many sheep can you stuff in the cargo compartment of a 1962 Checker Marathon station wagon? Who cares? It makes for effective advertising of the spacious cargo area of the Checker wagon. You just wouldn't want to be the one who had to clean the car's interior after the photo shoot.

In 1966, the Checker Marathon station wagon could be ordered with a Chevrolet 327-cid V-8 engine. This factory illustration was a bit odd in that it depicted the car, rigged for towing a travel trailer, with whitewall tires only on the front. Checker's penchant for finding unusual ways to promote the Marathon wagon's ample cargo space continued in 1966. That year it was promoted via three lads stretched out and playing with a slot car track set up in the rear compartment. Hey, Mom, shouldn't you be watching the road?

Studebaker

While it never reached production, Studebaker built a prototype Champion station wagon in 1947, designed by Raymond Loewy. The prototype wagon featured sliding glass windows in both its rear doors and quarters. Note the difference between the rear roof line of the prototype (above) compared to an early Loewy rendering of the car (below).

Studebaker returned to station wagon production in 1954 offering four different two-door models, two each in the Champion and Commander series. Cleverly posed with an old Conestoga wagon, this was Studebaker's Commander Deluxe Conestoga station wagon. Its price was $2,448 and 1,912 were produced. The Conestoga featured roll-up windows in the front doors and sliding glass in the center windows only.

The 1956 Studebaker President Pinehurst two-door station wagon was priced at $2,529. Production of the six-passenger wagon totaled 1,522. This was Studebaker's top-line wagon for 1956 and it offered 65 cubic feet of cargo space.

In both 1957 and 1958, Studebaker offered the economical Scotsman station wagon. It was unique in that it was a "plain-Jane" model devoid of all chrome except the bumpers and equally spartan on the inside. More than 11,000 of the two-door wagons were built in the two years it was available.

The top-line station wagon offered by Studebaker in 1957 was the President Broadmoor, the first four-door wagon for Studebaker since 1939. Twin Traction limited slip differential and an air mattress were optional equipment as was the roof rack pictured. Price of the Broadmoor was $2,666 and 1,530 were built.

In 1959, Studebaker introduced its compact Lark models. Included in the Lark lineup was the Deluxe station wagon, identified by its body color headlight rims compared to the top-line Regal's chrome rims. Both Deluxe and Regal wagons (all two-door models) were offered with six-cylinder (VI) and V-8 (VIII) engines. This six-cylinder-powered Deluxe was priced at $2,295 and production totaled 13,227. The compact Lark wagon offered 93 cubic feet of cargo space.

As of 1962, Studebaker Lark station wagons were available only as four-door models. The roof rack depicted was a $54 option. For an additional $124, a third seat could be ordered for the Lark wagon, which included Captive-Air tires and no spare. Again, the Lark wagon was available as either a Deluxe or Regal model with six-cylinder or V-8 engine.

A revolutionary although never imitated innovation was the Brooks Stevens-designed Studebaker Daytona Wagonaire station wagon with the sliding roof panel. The 1965 Wagonaire was only available with the sliding panel as opposed to other years when a fixed-top version was also offered. Note in the photo with the Daytona's tailgate down the optional one-rung step that folded into the tailgate. Price of this Wagonaire was $2,890 and only 723 were produced. Power was supplied by a 283-cid Chevrolet V-8.

Chrysler

Lacking the wood so common on earlier Chrysler Town & Country station wagons, this 1955 Windsor Deluxe Town & Country relied instead on Virgil Exner's new "100 Million Dollar Look" design. The "V" on the gastank filler lid signified the 301-cid V-8 powering all Windsor Deluxes that year. Price of this wagon was $3,331. Production totaled 1,983.

Marketed as "A Luxury Car Made Into a Wagon," the 1970 Chrysler Town & Country station wagon, offered in both six- and nine-passenger versions, was a separate series for the second year in-a-row. Featuring simulated Brazilian Rosewood appliqué, double-action tailgate and 113 cubic feet of cargo space (in two-seat version), the T&C was priced at $5,349 (six-passenger) and $5,435 (nine-passenger). Production totaled 5,686 and 9,583, respectively.

Chrysler's move to smaller station wagons began with the dropping in 1978 of the large Town & Country wagons. The T&C name was carried over to the 112.7-inch wheelbase LeBaron series station wagon that featured simulated wood exterior treatment. Six-passenger T&C production totaled 21,504 for both the six-cylinder-powered version ($5,672) and V-8-powered version ($5,848).

DeSoto

The body shell of the 1953 DeSoto Firedome station wagon was shared with Chrysler. The V-8 symbols on the front fenders signified the 276-cid engine. The front and rear doors contained vent windows. Price was $3,366 and 1,100 Firedome wagons were built that year.

The second-to-last year that DeSoto would offer a station wagon, the 1958 DeSoto Firesweep Explorer was one of four wagons produced that year in the Firesweep (two models) and Fireflite (two models) series. The Firesweep Explorer was available as a six-passenger wagon for $3,266 or as a nine-passenger wagon for $3,408. Production figures were 1,305 and 1,125, respectively. The whitewall tires were a $45 option.

Dodge

Introduced midway through 1949, the Dodge Coronet station wagon was part of the top-line Dodge offerings that year. Featuring wood framing with mahogany panel appliqué, the three-seat, eight-passenger wagon's roof was all-steel and the rear doors had sliding glass windows. This was Dodge's first station wagon since 1938. Only 800 of these Coronet wagons were produced, priced at $2,865 each.

The 1954 Dodge Coronet Sierra station wagon arrived in dealer showrooms in December of 1953. The 119-inch wheelbase Sierra seated eight-passengers in its three-seat configuration (it was also offered in a two-seat, six-passenger configuration). Power was supplied from either a six-cylinder engine or Hemi V-8. Price of the Sierra was $2,694 and $2,935, respectively. Production of both versions totaled 1,300.

Continuing the "Swept Wing" styling introduced in 1957, this 1958 Custom Sierra was the top-line station wagon for Dodge. Offered in six- and nine-passenger configurations, the Custom Sierra featured a spare tire that was mounted behind the right rear wheel and was accessible from a removable fender skirt located behind the rear wheelwell. The rear-facing third seat in the nine-passenger model was called a "spectator" seat.

Dodge introduced new styling in 1966, and that year's Coronet series is now considered by many car enthusiasts to be the most attractive of that model's entire run. This Coronet Deluxe station wagon had a wheelbase of 117 inches and was available only in a two-seat, six-passenger configuration.

Dodge's top-line station wagon for 1971 was the Coronet Crestwood, offered in both six- and nine-passenger versions. It featured woodgrain appliqué, and the variable-opening doorgate and rear window wind deflector were standard equipment. Price and production total were $3,601 and 2,884, respectively, for the six-passenger model and $3,682 and 3,981, respectively, for the nine-passenger Crestwood.

The 1975 Dodge Coronet Custom station wagon was available as a six-passenger model ($4,560) or nine-passenger model ($4,674). In the two views (below) of the rear compartment, both the amount of cargo space and the rear-facing third seat of the nine-passenger wagon were promoted. The Custom was Coronet's mid-level wagon in 1975.

Ford

Designed to compete with the Chevy Nomad, Ford offered this stylish two-door 1957 Del Rio Ranch Wagon which outsold the Nomad almost 8:1. This black beauty — complete with sliding glass panels in the rear quarter windows — is owned by William Ursprung Jr. of Palmyra, Pa. It was used as a backup delivery vehicle for a florist for 10 years, and was then stored from 1968 to 1986. Other than new paint and some new old stock interior pieces, the car is original. (Photos courtesy of William Ursprung Jr.)

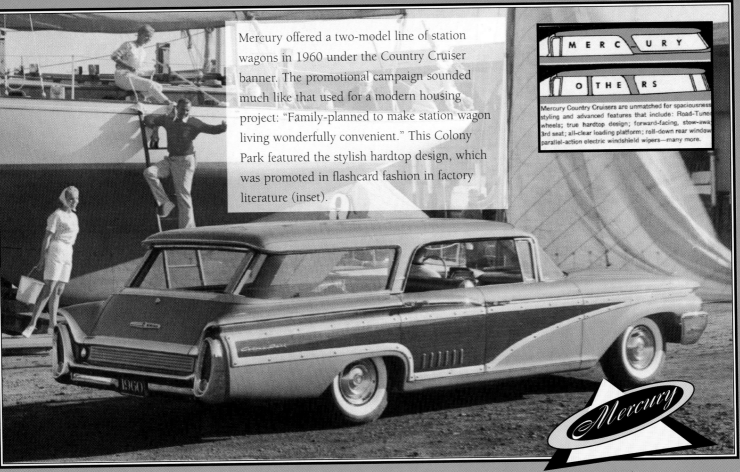

Mercury offered a two-model line of station wagons in 1960 under the Country Cruiser banner. The promotional campaign sounded much like that used for a modern housing project: "Family-planned to make station wagon living wonderfully convenient." This Colony Park featured the stylish hardtop design, which was promoted in flashcard fashion in factory literature (inset).

MERCURY OTHERS

Mercury Country Cruisers are unmatched for spaciousness styling and advanced features that include: Road-Tuned wheels; true hardtop design; forward-facing, stow-away 3rd seat; all-clear loading platform; roll-down rear window; parallel-action electric windshield wipers—many more.

Mercury

After abandoning the station wagon market after the 1950 model year, Oldsmobile returned to station wagon production in 1957 with several models including this Golden Rocket 88 Fiesta "sedan." Strangely, the Golden Rocket name — for Olds' base 88 series — designated General Motors' 50th Anniversary, not Oldsmobile's, which was observed 10 years earlier. Also, naming a car that is clearly a station wagon a "sedan" was to differentiate this model from the hardtop Fiesta station wagon.

Promoted as the "sky's-the-limit look," the distinctive Vista Roof was a popular Oldsmobile offering as seen on this 1965 Olds Custom Vista Cruiser station wagon. Powered by the Jetfire Rocket V-8 engine, this Vista Cruiser featured 100 cubic feet of cargo capacity. Also, it was available in two-seat and three-seat configurations, with the third seat a forward-facing setup.

Dressed up in the optional XC special edition package, this 1990 Oldsmobile Custom Cruiser was the lone rear-drive V-8-powered offering for Olds that year. Entering its third decade of production, the Custom Cruiser — which debuted in 1971 — was powered by a 5.0-liter (307-cid) V-8 and rode on a 116-inch wheelbase (220-inch overall length).

A 1941 Packard 110 Deluxe station wagon. This eight-passenger, wood-bodied beauty was powered by an inline six-cylinder engine rated at 245 cid and 100 hp.

A member of the 19th Series Packard lineup, this Junior Packard featured the new — for 1941— Electromatic semi-automatic clutch.

Promoted in factory literature as the successor to the station wagon, this beautiful wood-bodied 1948 Packard Station Sedan featured a 120-inch wheelbase. Fine-grained hardwoods made up the side and rear panels.

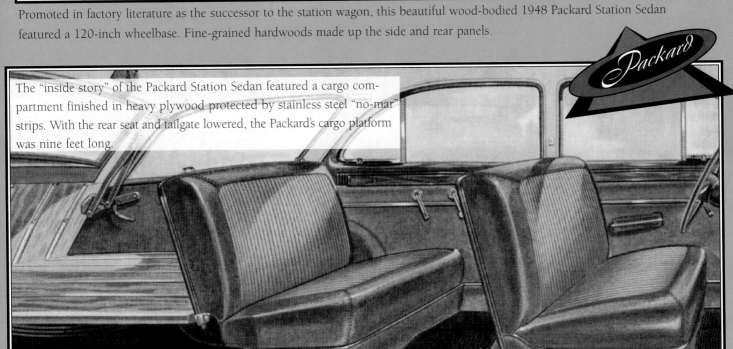

The "inside story" of the Packard Station Sedan featured a cargo compartment finished in heavy plywood protected by stainless steel "no-mar" strips. With the rear seat and tailgate lowered, the Packard's cargo platform was nine feet long.

Call it a "Georgia Peach" or jewel-in-the-rough, but when Michael Pearson purchased this 1959 Plymouth Custom Suburban station wagon from an Atlanta family that had owned it since new it had less than 30,000 miles on it. That was in 1994, and since then Pearson has done some work on the car, which was parked in 1972 and suffered cosmetic damage in the ensuing years of neglect. All those state decals in the rear window reflect the amount of miles this Plymouth has traveled.

Optional equipment was offered to dress-up your Pontiac, as evidenced by this 1966 Bonneville station wagon in an artist's rendering in factory literature. This Bonneville featured optional Cordova vinyl roof covering, roof rack and popular aluminum brake drum with integral hub, more commonly referred to as eight-lug wheels.

Equipped with a siren and rail wheels front and rear, this 1957 Pontiac Super Chief Safari station wagon makes a safety run on tracks in Newport, Michigan, with the Enrico Fermi-Detroit Edison power plant in the background. Railroads often used station wagons for track maintenance duties based on both their crew and cargo carrying capabilities. (Photo courtesy of E.V. Schwandt)

Arnie "The Farmer" Beswick drag raced this 1963 Pontiac Tempest station wagon, named "Mrs. B's Famous Grocery Getter," in the Stock Eliminator class during the mid-1960s. The unique racer was one of six factory lightweight Tempest wagons produced by General Motors in 1963. It was powered by a 421-cid Super Duty V-8 engine, and featured an aluminum front end. Vintage drag racing artist Tim Frederick of Maryland has recreated the 'Grocery Getter' at speed on the quarter-mile.

A 1962 Rambler Ambassador 400 station wagon with fifth door in back that swings open a wide 90 degrees for convenient access to the extra-seating and cargo areas. This Ambassador was powered by a 327-cid/250-hp V-8. Interior appointments included a padded dash, robe rail and electric clock while outside the roof-mounted travel rack was standard equipment.

"The Most Versatile Wagon on Wheels" was how Studebaker promoted it's 1963 Lark Daytona Wagonaire. With its rear sliding roof, the Wagonaire was a three-in-one wonder: a stylish family car, a functional utility wagon, and a fun-filled convertible (never mind that the wind-in-your-hair sensation was coming from behind). Note the optional one-rung folding ladder on the tailgate.

AMC

One of the unique last-gasp products of American Motors Corp., the four-wheel-drive Eagle station wagon has earned a genuine cult following among auto enthusiasts. This 1988 model was one of the last Eagle station wagons produced in late 1987 in Brampton, Ontario, Canada, after AMC had been taken over by Chrysler. The woodgrain side panels, roof rack and wire wheel covers were optional equipment.

America's smartest new, double-duty automobiles!

Versatile **Edsel** Station Wagons for **1959**

All aboard for active living

Sales Literature

Rambler Station Wagons For **1962**

American - Classic - Ambassador

1971 **Plymouth** Station Wagons

Coming Through

The 1990 Oldsmobile Expression concept car, while possessing all the attributes of a station wagon, was referred to as a Family Sport Sedan. This artist rendering of the car is different from the all-pearlescent red-orange finish of the Expression that debuted at the 1990 Chicago Auto Show.

Concept Cars

The Expression's two rear-facing seats face a tailgate that doubles as an entertainment center with a video game center, VCR, storage center and built-in vacuum cleaner.

Overhead artist rendering shows an all-leather interior in sable and tan with orange piping, with seating for six.

The Expression's cockpit-like driv compartment features a hands-off cellu phone and console-mounted CRT scre with a navigational system as well steering wheel touch controls for sou and ventilation syster

Station Wagon Collectibles

Scale Model Products 1958 Chevrolet Nomad station wagon, dealer promotional, no interior.

Johan 1961 Rambler Classic Custom Cross Country station wagon, dealer promotional with friction motor.

Product Miniature Company 1956 Ford Country Sedan station wagon, dealer promotional, tinted windows.

Corgi #445 1959 Plymouth Sport

Suburban station wagon, yellow interior.

Buddy L Suburban station wagon and TeePee pop-up camper set #5359, issued in 1963. Camping trailer features a plastic folding tent and bed on a steel trailer.
Station wagon is equipped with spring suspension.

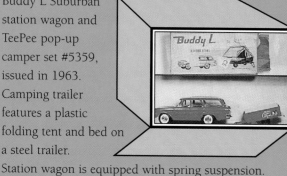

Matchbox #73 1969 Mercury 'Commuter' station wagon.

A pair die-cas Tootsie station wagon #1046, originally issued in 1940 (reissued after World War #239, issued in 1947.

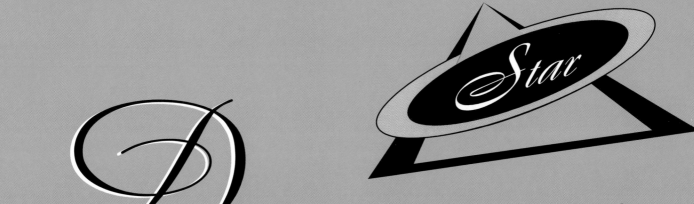

*D*isagreement exists among auto historians as to which manufacturer produced the first "true" station wagon. One of the earliest versions belongs to Star, a low-priced line of cars introduced in 1922 by William Crapo Durant to compete with Henry Ford's Model T. History records the 1924 Star (pictured) as "the first major American car to offer station wagon styling from the factory." While this model is pictured with two seats, a third, forward-facing seat could be installed in the rear. (Photo courtesy of Long Island Auto Museum)

Jim and Mary Jaeger of Buffalo, Minn., are the owners of this 'before-and-after' Buick, a 1956 Century station wagon they have named "Petunia." The inset photo shows the before version, purchased for $150 in rough and rusty condition. The after shows the restored version, in black, coral and white colors, which has ferried the Jaegers on several vacation trips and to and from Buick Club of America meets. (Photos courtesy of Jim Jaeger)

What many consider to be the last "true" American station wagon, the 1996 Buick Roadmaster Estate Wagon. Along with the Chevrolet Caprice Classic station wagon of that year, Detroit halted production of these two remaining rear-drive, long wheelbase wagons — ending almost 70 years (not counting World War II) of wagon production. Station wagons such as the Roadmaster and Caprice fell victim to the emergence of both the minivan and sport utility vehicle as the vehicles of choice for families and travelers.

Stunning in a vibrant red finish, this 1970 Checker Marathon station wagon was promoted in factory literature as having over 93 cubic feet of storage space. This less-than-17-foot-long Marathon could accommodate 4x8 sheets of plywood, which is as close to a "woodie" model as Checker would get.

Chevy

"Just a tired old Chevy" is how owner Ken Buttolph (*Old Cars Price Guide* and *Old Cars Weekly News & Marketplace* editor) describes his 1947 Chevrolet Fleetmaster wood-bodied station wagon. Ken found this car in 1967, parked with wheels removed, during one of his legendary forays to a salvage yard, this one located in Oshkosh, Wis. He started the Chevy and thought the six-cylinder engine ran "pretty good," so he scrounged around and found a jack, wheels and lugnuts and commenced to making the "woodie" roadworthy again. The car had approximately 70,000 miles on it, but Ken said the interior was still in good shape. After a bit of haggling with the salvage yard's owner, Ken drove away in his $65 acquisition. After driving the car for two years and adding about 8,000 miles to the odometer, Ken traded the Chevy wagon at a dealership for a 1953 Chevrolet coupe, which he still owns today.

Apart from a new paint job and a thorough cleaning, this is an original 1960 Chevrolet Nomad station wagon. A member of the top trim level Impala series, this Nomad features the one-year-only gas tank location under the rear seat.

Owner Greg Englin of Illinois purchased the car with 104,000 miles on it. All the original-dealer stickers are proudly displayed in the rear windows. Englin said he and his family drive the Nomad everywhere, adding, "Trailers are for horses!" The Nomad was no lightweight, though, weighing in at a hefty 3,955 pounds with 348-cid V-8 and Turboglide transmission.

Chevy

Crocus yellow and Laurel green are the colors of this two-toned 1956 Chevrolet Two-Ten Beauville station wagon. The Beauville was equipped with a third seat and accommodated nine passengers. With the two rear seats and tailgate lowered, that Soap Box Derby racer could ride in the back quite nicely.

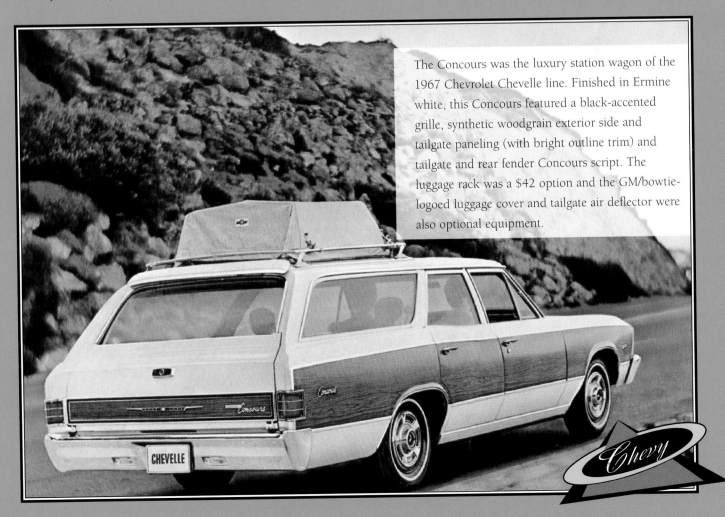

The Concours was the luxury station wagon of the 1967 Chevrolet Chevelle line. Finished in Ermine white, this Concours featured a black-accented grille, synthetic woodgrain exterior side and tailgate paneling (with bright outline trim) and tailgate and rear fender Concours script. The luggage rack was a $42 option and the GM/bowtie-logoed luggage cover and tailgate air deflector were also optional equipment.

Two versions of the 1950 Chrysler Royal station wagon were offered, one being an all-steel model and the other version the steel-bodied car with ash trim bolted on such as the car pictured. Part way through production of this wagon, Chrysler added Town & Country to the Royal name. Only 599 of these Royal 'woodies' were produced that year (compared to a paltry 99 of the all-steel version).

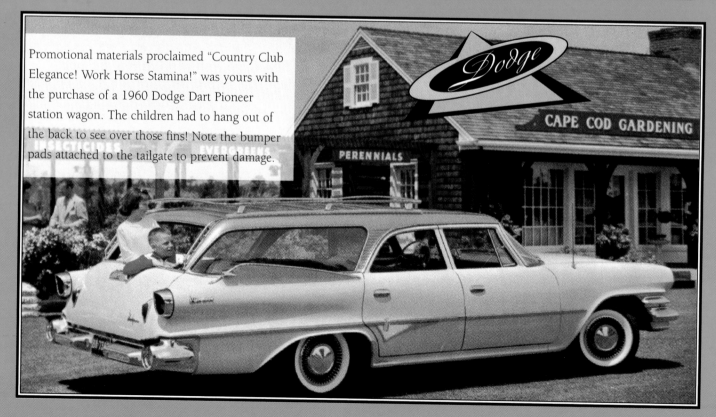

Promotional materials proclaimed "Country Club Elegance! Work Horse Stamina!" was yours with the purchase of a 1960 Dodge Dart Pioneer station wagon. The children had to hang out of the back to see over those fins! Note the bumper pads attached to the tailgate to prevent damage.

Only 1,083 1955 DeSoto Firedome station wagons were produced, with the model being the heaviest (4,175 pounds) and costliest ($3,170) of the DeSoto lineup that year. Having seen one new in a dealership at age 14 is what prompted Dorsey Lewis of Milwaukie, Ore., to rescue this Firedome from a cow pasture and expend three years of "blood, sweat and $$$" returning it to better-than-new condition. A view of the cargo area shows the detail of the restoration project. The woman posing with the Firedome (inset) is not identified but she and the DeSoto look tiny compared to those trees in the background!

DeSoto

Dodge

A 1961 Dodge Seneca station wagon photographed in Letchworth State Park in New York. The Seneca featured unibody construction, which was uncommon for a large car of that period (122-inch wheelbase). The Seneca offered push-button transmission, heater/defroster and radio controls. Also, note the reversal in fin styling from the year previous.

Available in only the Super Deluxe series, the 1946 Ford wood-bodied station wagon could be had with either the 226-cid inline six or 239-cid V-8. This restored "woodie" features an optional cowl-mounted spotlight and front-mounted fog lights. Also, the right swing-down taillight was optional as these cars came standard only with the left taillight. The rear forward-facing seat and center seat could be removed to increase cargo capacity.

The "wood" and white combination dressing this 1955 Mercury Monterey station wagon is a real eye-catcher. New on this model were the Full-Scope windshield and Super-Torque V-8 equipped with four-barrel carburetor and dual exhaust.

The Monterey's interior could be ordered in green, blue or this red vinyl with "harmonizing Chromatex." Standard equipment included coat hooks, interior courtesy lights and the always handy robe cord. The gifts were optional.

One of the new option packages available for the 1979 Dodge Aspen line was the Sport Wagon package. It enhanced the base Aspen station wagon with flared wheel openings, bucket seats and aluminum wheels. The five-passenger wagon also featured thick pin striping and a roof rack with the $630 package. Wheelbase of the Aspen station wagon was 112.7 inches.

Plymouth

Relatively unchanged from 1946 to 1948, this Plymouth Special Deluxe station wagon achieved a production total of 12,913 in that time. The P-15 series wagon's price increased from $1,539 in 1946 to $2,068 in 1948. The wood body of this three-seat, eight-passenger wagon was either mahogany or light maple panels, crafted by U.S. Body & Forging Co. for Plymouth. This wagon featured white wheel trim rings and sliding glass in the rear door and quarter windows.

Popularly regarded as the automobile industry's first all-steel station wagon, the 1949 Plymouth Deluxe Suburban two-door station wagon was a departure from the traditional wood-bodied wagons. This particular P-17 series wagon was a model released early (after a late introduction in March 1949) lacking the proper front fender Deluxe script and the at-first-optional-and-later-standard rear fender trim spear. The five-passenger Suburban featured a two-piece tailgate and sliding glass windows between the B- and C-pillars. It was marketed as "The Car With 101 Uses" and was priced at $1,840. Production totaled 19,220. The whitewall tires were an option.

Displayed at an auto show, this 1954 Plymouth Belvedere Suburban two-door station wagon sported optional ($59.15) wire wheel covers. The six-passenger wagon featured sliding glass windows between the B- and C-pillars and a "dressy" interior composed of pleated vinyl and basket weave vinyl. Price was $2,268 and production totaled 9,241.

Representing the base level offering that year, the 1955 Plymouth Plaza Suburban station wagon did not appear in dealer showrooms until December of 1954. Available with six-cylinder power ($2,133) or V-8 engine ($2,237), production for both versions totaled 15,442. At mid-model year, the side spear trim depicted was offered as optional equipment and a one-piece plastic headliner was installed in all Plymouth Suburbans as a no-cost addition.

The compact Valiant series was introduced in 1960. Oddly, in this first year, Valiants were assembled by the Dodge Division but marketed through Plymouth dealers. Valiants carried no marque identification, being promoted by Chrysler Corp. as a separate series. Within the line, there were four Suburban station wagons, two each in the V-100 and V-200 lines. This 106.5-inch wheelbase wagon was the base V-100 Suburban, available in either six-passenger ($2,365) or nine-passenger ($2,488) configurations. Production totaled 12,018 and 1,928, respectively. The whitewall tires were a $29 option and a power tailgate window could be ordered for an additional $33. A Dodge Power Wagon firetruck appeared in the background.

Plymouth's larger station wagon offering for 1960 was the Sport Suburban, its top-line wagon for that year. Even with a 122-inch wheelbase, this large car featured unibody construction as well as a unique rectangular Aero (steering) Wheel for easing the driver's entry into and exit from the car. The Sport Suburban was offered as a six-passenger model or this nine-passenger version with a rear-facing third seat. On this Sport Suburban a power tailgate window and D-pillar assist handles were standard equipment. Price of the Sport Suburban was $2,989 (six-passenger) and $3,099 (nine-passenger) while production totaled 3,333 and 4,253, respectively.

For 1965, Plymouth offered three trim levels of station wagons in its Fury line: base, Fury II and Fury III. This Fury III wagon was the top trim level and was offered in six- and nine-passenger configurations. The roof rack was optional equipment. Price of the Fury III six-passenger wagon was $3,047 and 8,931 were built while the nine-passenger model cost $3,148 and 9,546 were built.

This Plymouth station wagon is the perfect example of how marketing drives the auto industry. Obviously a pre-model year press release photo, the tailgate script on this 1971 wagon reads Plymouth Belvedere Sport. In reality, no such model existed in the Plymouth line for 1971 so last minute changes in naming models must have occurred. What this car represents is the 1971 Plymouth Satellite Regent six-passenger wagon, priced at $3,558. A nine-passenger version was also available for $3,638. Production totals were 2,161 and 2,985, respectively. The interior view (lower photo) promoted the storage bins molded into the plastic wheelhouse covers.

Introduced in 1976 as a replacement for the long-running Valiant series, the Plymouth Volare station wagon was offered in two trim levels: base (above) and Premier (below, in see-through rendering). Both Volare wagons were six-passenger models riding on a 112.5-inch wheelbase, and offered 71.9 cubic feet of cargo space. Both were available with six-cylinder or V-8 engines. The Premier wagon featured woodgrain appliqué. The roof rack and air deflector were optional equipment at $65 and $22, respectively. Production totaled 40,497 for six-cylinder and V-8 versions of the base Volare and 44,191 for both models of the Premier.

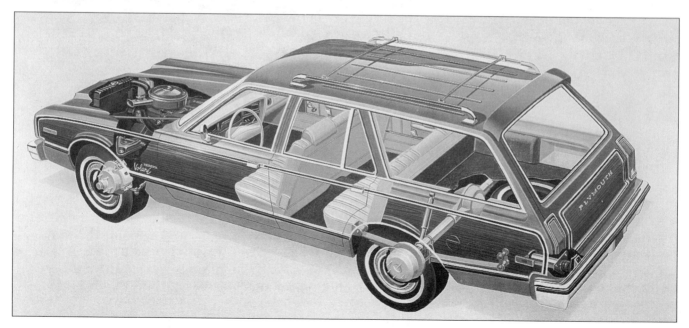

Edsel

Factory literature for the 1959 Edsel Villager station wagon reads in part: "You get a big car without a wasted inch of useless length." The Villager's measurements were a 118-inch wheelbase within a 210.1-inch overall length. Available in both six- and nine-passenger configurations, the price of the Villager was $2,971 and $3,055, respectively. Production totaled 5,687 (six-passenger) and 2,133 (nine-passenger). The rooftop carrier was optional equipment.

Ford

The boy peeking out of this 1949 Ford Custom two-door station wagon helped promote the sliding glass in the wagon's quarter windows. Ford only offered two-door wagons in 1949. They featured an all-steel top and steel sub-framing covered with decorative wood. Production of this eight-passenger "woodie" totaled 31,412 in both six-cylinder and V-8 versions. Due to this wagon's steel top, headliners were offered in 1949 Ford wagons for the first time.

The 1951 Ford Custom Deluxe two-door station wagon was the last Ford wagon to feature structural wood in its design and the first to carry the Country Squire name. Offered in both six-cylinder and V-8 versions, production totaled 29,617 including both versions. This eight-passenger "woodie" was badged as having V-8 power. Due to the 1950 closing of Ford's wagon assembly plant in Iron Mountain, Mich., the 1951 Country Squires were constructed by the Ionia Body Co.

The newly styled, all-steel 1952 Ford Ranch Wagon was part of the base trim level Mainline series. Of the three series of Ford station wagons offered in 1952, this was the only two-door model available. Priced at $1,832 with six-cylinder power and $1,902 with a V-8, production of both totaled 32,566. The six-passenger wagon's rear quarter windows featured sliding glass. Note the scissor-hinges used on the rear two-piece liftgate.

Ford's mid-level trim station wagon in 1954 was the Customline Country Sedan. It could be ordered in either six-passenger or eight-passenger configurations with either six-cylinder or V-8 power. Total production of all versions of the Country Sedan was 48,384. The rear doors contained non-movable "vent" panes while the rear quarter windows featured sliding glass. The two-tone finish depicted was optional.

Beginning in 1955, Ford classed its station wagons as a separate series. This 1956 Ford Country Squire was the top-line wagon Ford offered and the only one available with simulated (fiberglass framing over decal paper) wood trim. The three-seat, eight-passenger wagon could be ordered with six-cylinder or V-8 powerplant. A total of 23,221 were built including both engine versions. The whitewall tires were optional.

This 1957 Ford Country Sedan station wagon was Ford's mid-level trim offering in its wagon series. This three-seat, nine-passenger model was priced at $2,556 with six-cylinder engine and $2,656 with a V-8. Production of both models totaled 49,638. The Country Sedan was also available in a two-seat, six-passenger configuration. A new sliding latch support debuted on all 1957 Ford wagons' liftgates, replacing the former scissor-hinge arrangement.

Beginning in 1958, Ford's base trim level Ranch Wagon was available as both a two-door and four-door model. Both versions seated six. This two-door model cost $2,372 with six-cylinder power and $2,479 with a V-8. Production of both versions totaled 34,578 (32,854 of the four-door Ranch Wagons were sold in their debut offering). The whitewall tires were optional.

This 1959 Ford Country Sedan was the mid-level trim offering in that year's station wagon series. It was available in both two- and four-door versions, six- and nine-passenger configurations, and with six-cylinder or V-8 power. The six-passenger Country Sedan four-door model outsold the nine-passenger version 94,601 to 28,881. The "Styletone" two-tone paint on this wagon was a $26 option.

Ford introduced this compact two-door Falcon station wagon in 1960. This wagon featured the $66 Deluxe trim package. A total of 27,552 two-door Falcon wagons were produced that year, all with the six-cylinder engine, and with a base price of $2,225. The six-passenger Falcon wagon was the first Ford to feature a single-piece tailgate with retractable rear window.

New for 1962, and available only in the Deluxe Falcon series, was the six-passenger Squire station wagon with imitation wood trim. Optional equipment for this wagon included the $39 roof rack depicted and a $120 sport package that featured bucket seats and console. Base price of the Squire was $2,603 and 22,583 were built.

Remaining as Ford's top-line station wagon was the Country Squire. This three-seat, nine-passenger 1963 Country Squire was also offered in a two-seat, six-passenger version. Debate exists as to when (if?) it happened, but at some point for the 1963 model run the Country Squire was upgraded to be associated with the XL series. Production of the nine-passenger wagon totaled 19,246 in both six-cylinder and V-8 versions. After its "partnership" with the XL series, 437 Country Squires were produced with bucket seats and seating for five and 321 were built with bucket seats and seating for eight.

Available in six-passenger form only was the 1964 Ford Fairlane 500 Custom station wagon. It was offered with six-cylinder or V-8 power and 24,962 were built including both versions. The power tailgate window on this wagon was a $32 option. The suitcase shown was being loaded into the Custom wagon's sub-cargo floor storage compartment.

Badged as having the $246 optional big-block 390-cid V-8, this 1964 Ford Country Squire station wagon featured three seats and room for nine passengers. A two-seat, six-passenger version was also available. A total of 23,120 Country Squires were built in nine-passenger configuration, including both six-cylinder and V-8 versions. The power tailgate window was a $32 option.

New to Ford's 1967 Falcon Futura station wagon was the "Magic Doorgate" that could be set down or swung open as shown. The Futura wagon cost $2,609 and 4,552 were produced. The roof rack depicted was a $45 option. The vent-type windows in the rear doors were non-operational.

This 1967 Ford Country Squire station wagon was badged as having the optional 428-cid/345-hp big-block V-8. Available in both six- and nine-passenger configurations, the latter version featured dual center facing rear seats. The luggage rack shown was a $44 option or a Deluxe adjustable rack could be ordered for $63. The nine-passenger Country Squire cost $3,466 with a V-8 and 44,024 were pro-duced including six-cylinder and V-8 versions.

In its second year of availability in 1972, the Ford Pinto line introduced this two-door station wagon, which immediately found 101,483 buyers. This version of the four-passenger Pinto wagon included the optional Squire Package featuring simulated wood trim. The roof rack was also optional. Price of the base Pinto wagon was $2,265 and it was offered only with four-cylinder power. The Pinto wagon offered 60.5 cubic feet of cargo space.

Ford's "Magic Doorgate" became a standard feature on the 1973 Gran Torino Squire station wagon. Available only with a V-8, price of this 118-inch wheelbase wagon was $3,486 and 35,595 were built. A power tailgate window was a $34 option and the luggage rack depicted was a $77 option.

Base engine in the 1973 Ford LTD Country Squire station wagon was the 400-cid V-8. This was one of Ford's most popular selling station wagons with 142,933 produced. Price was $4,401. The power tailgate window and power front disc brakes were standard on this wagon. The roof rack and rear window wind deflector were optional as was the (lower photo) recreation table that fit between the LTD wagon's dual center facing rear seats. A vinyl roof was also offered as a $148 option.

Ford totally redesigned its LTD line for 1979. This LTD Country Squire wagon offered 91.7 cubic feet of cargo space and was the only LTD wagon to be offered with quad headlights set horizontally. The Country Squire was considered a $758 option package in addition to the LTD wagon's base price of $6,122. It was odd that Ford kept production figures for the "optional" Country Squire as 29,932 were built. Optional equipment depicted on this wagon included the $113 luggage rack and $145 wire wheel covers. For $149, dual center facing rear seats were also available.

The 1991 Ford LTD Crown Victoria Country Squire was the final Country Squire produced, ending 40 years of tradition as Ford's prestige station wagon. Introduced in 1951 as a two-door "woodie" model, the Country Squire evolved into this final version powered by a 5.0-liter (302-cid) V-8 and offered in base ($18,335) six-passenger or LX ($19,085) eight-passenger configurations.

Mercury

Fitted for ambulance duty at the Lincoln-Mercury Division Medical Department in Detroit, this 1948 Mercury station wagon, in stock form, was priced at $2,207 and 1,889 were produced. That year's wagons were near identical to the previous year's model. The 1948 wagon was Mercury's final wood-bodied model. The following year, an all-new, steel-bodied wagon was introduced. This eight-passenger "woodie" rode on a 118-inch wheelbase and 201.8-inch overall length.

Sharing its body shell with Ford, the 1949 Mercury station wagon was, nonetheless, an all-new design. The eight-passenger wagon featured a structural steel body with maple framing bolted on over mahogany panels. Price was $2,716 and 8,044 were produced. Sliding glass was featured in the rear quarter windows and the second and third seats were removable to gain additional cargo space. The whitewall tires were optional.

In 1953, Mercury reduced its station wagon line to one offering and elevated this wagon to its top-line, V-8-powered Monterey series. The eight-passenger Monterey wagon was priced at $2,591 and featured wood framing over simulated (decal) paneling. Production totaled 7,719. The whitewall tires were optional.

In 1957, Mercury began classing its station wagons as a separate series. This privately-owned six-passenger Voyager two-door hardtop station wagon featured the optional Quadri-Beam Headlamp setup (still illegal in some states in 1957) and modern tires. The Voyager was the mid-level trim wagon, above the Commuter and below the Colony Park. Only V-8 power was offered. Price of the Voyager two-door wagon was $3,403 and 2,283 were built.

Of Mercury's two-line station wagon series in 1964, this Colony Park was the top-line offering above the Commuter. This Colony Park was the three-seat, nine-passenger version priced at $3,504. Production totaled 5,624. The luggage rack shown was a $65 option. Colony Parks were offered only with V-8 power.

The 1966 Mercury Comet Villager station wagon was the top-line Comet wagon and featured simulated wood trim. This six-passenger wagon featured the $65 optional luggage rack. A power tailgate window was also available as a $30 option. Villagers came standard with the 200-cid six-cylinder engine. Price was $2,780 and 3,880 were produced.

This 1966 Mercury Colony Park station wagon was fitted with the optional $75 rear-facing third seat and $65 luggage rack. The 119-inch wheelbase wagon was base priced at $3,502 and 18,894 were built. The Colony Park offered only V-8 power.

Described when new as the "Lincoln Continental of station wagons," this 1968 Mercury Colony Park wagon was the top-line model of that year's two line (along with the Commuter) wagon series. Shown on this wagon was the optional $131 vinyl roof and $63 luggage rack. This two-seat, six-passenger Colony Park converted to a triple-seat configuration with the optional $126 rear-facing third seat. Dual center facing rear seats were also available as a $95 option. Base price of the V-8-powered Colony Park was $3,760 and 21,179 were built.

After several years of the Colony Park being offered only as a station wagon option package, the 1979 Mercury Marquis Colony Park wagon returned this long-standing name to regular production status. (Oddly, Mercury still listed the Colony Park package as a $586 option.) That year's Marquis was a totally new "downsized" design, some 17 inches shorter than the previous year's model. Standard features on this wagon included the 5.0-liter (302-cid) V-8, coach lamps and Deluxe wheel covers. The passenger capacity of the two-seat Colony Park was increased through the $193 optional dual center facing rear seats. The luggage rack shown was an $86 option. Base price of the wagon was $7,100 and 13,758 were produced.

The 1991 Mercury Grand Marquis Colony Park station wagon was the final time the Colony Park name was used to describe Mercury's prestige wagon, ending 35 years of tradition. This final Colony Park wagon was powered by the 5.0-liter (302-cid) V-8 and featured coach lamps and Deluxe wheel covers as standard equipment. The two-seat Colony Park featured over 90 cubic feet of cargo space with the second seat down.

Buick

The 1947 Buick Super Estate Wagon used a wood body supplied by Ionia. Unchanged from the previous year's styling, the Model 59 Super was powered by a straight-eight engine and featured a white Tenite steering wheel as standard equipment. The six-passenger Super Estate Wagon was priced at $2,594 and 786 were built.

Buick totally revamped the styling of its cars in 1949, including this six-passenger Super Estate Wagon. The only remaining large expanse of wood on this Super was its tailgate. The rear doors contained push-out vent windows, and the straight eight remained the Super's powerplant. Price was $3,178 and 1,830 were produced.

A new Buick series debuted in 1954, named the Century. Part of the Century lineup was an all-steel Estate Wagon, priced at $3,470. Production of the six-passenger Century totaled 1,563. Power was supplied by a V-8 engine. The Skylark wire wheels shown were an expensive and rare option. New for 1954 Buicks was the wraparound windshield.

The 1960 Buick Invicta Estate Wagon was available in both six- and nine-passenger configurations. Both versions featured wraparound windshields and rear quarter windows. This six-passenger Invicta was Buick's top-line wagon and cost $3,841. A total of 3,471 were built. The Invicta was powered by a V-8 engine.

In 1965, Buick offered two versions of its Special station wagon: standard and Deluxe models. This V-8-powered Special Deluxe six-passenger wagon featured an optional roof rack. Cost was $2,699 and 3,676 were built.

The lad with binoculars was promoting Buick's domed Skyroof design on this 1965 Skylark Custom Sport Wagon. Available in both six- and nine-passenger configurations, as well as a standard (non-Custom) version with both seating configurations, this six-passenger Skylark Custom Sport Wagon was priced at $3,092 and 8,300 were built. A tailgate lamp was standard equipment and with the rear seat folded down, this wagon offered 95.6 cubic feet of cargo space.

The Deluxe version of Buick's 1968 Sport Wagon featured simulated wood appliqué on its sides and tailgate. Available in both six- and nine-passenger configurations, the Sport Wagon featured the domed Skyroof design shared with Oldsmobile. The six-passenger model cost $3,711 and 4,614 were built. The nine-passenger version was priced at $3,869 and 6,295 were produced. Sport Wagons were based on a 121-inch wheelbase and offered up to 100 cubic feet of cargo space.

For the first time since 1964, in 1970, Buick marketed a "big" station wagon with its new Estate Wagon, available in six- and nine-passenger configurations. Featuring a 124-inch wheelbase and 223.3-inch overall length, the Sport Wagon had a dual action tail/door gate and simulated wood appliqué. Cost of the six-passenger version was $3,923 and 11,427 were produced. The nine-passenger Estate Wagon cost $4,068 and 16,879 were built.

This 1974 Buick Century Luxus station wagon featured the optional $136 simulated wood appliqué, $21 rear window air deflector and $64 luggage rack. The Century Luxus wagon was available in six- and nine-passenger versions and production of both totaled 6,791. Cost was $4,371 and $4,486, respectively. The Century Luxus used a hatch-type rear door.

While its Electra coupe and sedan counterparts went to front-wheel-drive and V-6 engine, the 1985 Buick Electra Estate Wagon retained rear-wheel-drive and V-8 power. Priced at $15,323, a total of 7,769 were built. The posh Electra Estate Wagon featured styled aluminum wheels, simulated wood appliqué and roof rack as standard fare and was available in six- and nine-passenger configurations.

Chevrolet

Chevrolet's mid-level station wagon for 1953 (above the 150 Special Handyman and below the 210 Deluxe Townsman) was the 210 Deluxe Handyman, finished in two-tone paint. Wagons were the only Chevy models in 1953 to have the exposed gas filler. The 210 Deluxe Handyman was available only in six-passenger format (the Townsman was the nine-passenger version). Price was $2,123 ($150 more for the Townsman) and 18,258 were produced (7,988 Townsman wagons were built). Only six-cylinder engines were available.

Displayed under the bright lights of an auto show, the 1955 Chevrolet Bel Air Nomad sport wagon was new and different. The six-passenger Nomad had features that were unique to the two-door wagon including: chrome headlight "eyebrows," a tailgate that allowed the rear window to be lowered instead of the conventional liftgate window and a ribbed roof panel. Production totaled 6,103 and power was supplied by a six-cylinder engine or the new-for-1955 265-cid V-8, Chevy's first V-8 since 1919.

The base Chevrolet series for 1957 was the 150, which included the two-door, six-passenger Handyman station wagon. The 150 Handyman featured an all-vinyl interior and minimal trim. Two-tone paint was optional. Price was $2,307 with a six-cylinder engine and $100 more for the V-8 version. Production totaled 14,740.

The top-line Chevrolet station wagon for 1957 was the Bel Air Townsman, available only as a six-passenger model. The Townsman and Nomad were the two station wagons available in 1957 in the Bel Air series. With six-cylinder power, the Bel Air Townsman cost $2,580 while a V-8 engine added $100. Production for both versions totaled 27,375. Unlike the Nomad, the Bel Air Townsman had a standard tailgate and liftgate window.

A case where the dog was almost as big as the car, in 1961, Chevrolet added a station wagon to its Corvair line. The Lakewood wagon was available as a base 500 series model or this Deluxe 700 series version. Both had six-passenger capacity, and were powered by an air-cooled, horizontally-opposed, aluminum-block six-cylinder engine located in the rear. With the rear seat folded down as shown, the dog had 58 cubic feet of space to roam around. Cost of the Lakewood 700 wagon was $2,330 and 20,451 were built. Figures for the Lakewood 500 wagon were $2,266 and 5,591, respectively.

Chevrolet's highest priced model for 1961 was the Nomad four-door station wagon, available in both six- and nine-passenger configurations, and part of the Impala series. This six-passenger model was priced at $2,996 (V-8 powered) with the nine-passenger version costing $103 more and including a power-operated tailgate window.

Chevrolet introduced its Chevy II line in 1962 to combat Ford's Falcon line of compact cars. The Chevy II line consisted of four series: 100, 200 (discontinued immediately after introduction), 300 and Nova 400. This 300 series station wagon was the mid-level offering above the 100 series wagon and below the Nova 400 model. The 300 series wagon was the only Chevy II offered in nine-passenger configuration (it could be ordered with rear-facing third seat deleted for a $70 credit). Power was supplied by either four- or six-cylinder engines with a factory kit for installation of a V-8 offered as an option. With the rear and third seats folded down, the Chevy II 300 series wagon had almost 77 cubic feet of cargo space.

Not since 1954 had a Chevrolet station wagon featured simulated "wood" trim, which made its return in 1966 exclusively on Chevy's top-line Caprice Custom station wagon, available in both six- and nine-passenger configurations. Available only with V-8 power, the six-passenger model was priced at $3,234 while the three-seat version cost $3,347. Dual seatbelts were standard equipment on all seats, including third-seat models. This Caprice Custom wagon was badged as having the 396-cid Turbo-Jet V-8.

The Concours model was introduced in 1967 as a luxury station wagon offering in Chevrolet's Chevelle line. This six-passenger wagon featured a black-accented grille, simulated wood appliqué, wheelhouse moldings, ribbed rocker panel moldings and rear fender script. Price of the Concours wagon was $2,827 with six-cylinder power and $2,933 with V-8 engine. The interior of the Concours was textured vinyl with full carpeting on passenger floors and vinyl coating on the cargo floor.

The top-line Chevrolet station wagon for 1974 was the Caprice Estate wagon, shown with the optional $77 luggage rack. Simulated wood appliqué and Chevy's "Clam Shell" tailgate were standard features of the Caprice Estate wagon. Only V-8 power was offered. The Caprice Estate wagon was available in both six- and nine-passenger configurations priced at $4,800 and $4,914, respectively.

In 1971, Chevrolet introduced its sub-compact Vega 2300 line to combat the foreign invasion of small cars. Part of the economy Vega series was the four-passenger Kammback sports wagon that rode on a 97-inch wheelbase. Power was supplied by an aluminum-block, overhead cam four-cylinder engine. The Vega Kammback featured a hatch-type rear door. Price was $2,328 and 42,800 were produced.

Chevrolet introduced a station wagon to its Caprice line in 1991, priced at $17,875. Standard equipment on the Caprice wagon included anti-lock brakes, driver's side airbag, air conditioning and power windows and power door locks. Power was supplied by a 5.0-liter V-8 with electronic fuel injection.

Oldsmobile

The 1948 Oldsmobile 66 series station wagon depicted (above) with the optional $30 Cadet Outside Visor installed and $10 chrome wheel trim rings. This wagon was Olds most expensive six-cylinder-powered offering, priced at $2,614. Production of the six-passenger wagon totaled 1,393 with the six-cylinder powerplant. The rear quarter windows contained sliding glass. The tailgate (below) was a two-piece unit with a hinged taillight attached. The 66 series wagon's interior was tan simulated leather, and the roof was fabric covered. The Olds wagon's body was supplied by Fisher Body Co.

There were actually four different station wagons offered by Oldsmobile in 1949 in the 76 and 88 series. Wood-bodied versions of the Futuramic 76 and 88 series wagons were available at the beginning of the model year. At mid-model year, new all-steel 76 and 88 series wagons with simulated wood trim became available. This six-cylinder-powered 76 wagon had an optional $30 Cadet Outside Visor installed and $10 chrome wheel trim rings. Production totaled 1,545 (both wood-bodied and all-steel-bodied) and the wagon's price was $2,735.

The 1959 Oldsmobile Super 88 Fiesta station wagon had eight more inches of cargo area than the previous year's model. The Super 88 Fiesta was Oldsmobile's top-line wagon model, and was priced at $3,669. Production totaled 7,015. This six-passenger wagon was available only with V-8 power.

Oldsmobile's top-line station wagon for 1961 was the Super 88 Fiesta, available in both six- and nine-passenger configurations (the latter with a rear facing third seat). A power-operated rear window was standard on the three-seat version and a $27 option on the two-seat model. Power was supplied by the 394-cid V-8 engine. Cost of the six-passenger Super 88 Fiesta wagon was $3,665 and 2,761 were built. For the nine-passenger version, the figures were $3,773 and 2,170, respectively.

Oldsmobile offered its 1964 Dynamic 88 Fiesta station wagon in both six- and nine-passenger configurations. This was the two-seat version, priced at $3,458. Production totaled 10,747. Options available for the Dynamic 88 Fiesta wagon included: power-operated rear window (standard on nine-passenger model), concealed and locking luggage compartment, divided second seat and a luggage rack. Only V-8 power was available.

Simulated wood appliqué was part of the package of the 1967 Oldsmobile Custom Vista Cruiser station wagon, available in both six- and nine-passenger versions. This Custom Vista Cruiser featured optional $68 wire wheel covers. Price of the six-passenger model was $3,228 and 9,513 were built. For the nine-passenger model, the figures were $3,339 and 15,293, respectively. All Vista Cruisers rode on an exclusive 120-inch wheelbase.

Oldsmobile introduced its full-size Custom Cruiser station wagon in 1971. The 127-inch wheelbase wagon came standard with a 455-cid V-8, and was available in six- and nine-passenger versions. General Motors' "Clam Shell" tailgate was used. Upholstery could be either vinyl or optional leather. Cost of the two-seat Custom Cruiser was $4,539 and 4,049 were produced. The price of the three-seat version was $4,680 and 9,932 were built.

After years of featuring the domed Skyroof (Buick's name) styling, in 1973, Oldsmobile switched to a Vista Vent (lower left photo) located at the front of the roof of its Vista Cruiser station wagon. The Vista Cruiser was based on an intermediate 116-inch wheelbase for 1973. Standard features included simulated wood appliqué and interior hood release. Also new-for-1973 was the "hatchgate" (lower right photo), which replaced the variable-opening tailgate formerly used. The roof rack depicted was optional. Price of the Vista Cruiser was $3,788 for the two-seat model and $3,901 for the three-seat version. Production figures were 10,894 and 13,531, respectively.

Oldsmobile's long-running Vista Cruiser station wagon continued in 1976, again available in two- and three-seat configurations. Simulated wood appliqué was standard, but the wire wheel covers depicted were a $120 option. The rear quarter windows featured operational vent "wings." Base powerplant was the 5.7-liter (350-cid) V-8. A "hatchgate" was used in the back. The two-seat Vista Cruiser cost $5,041 while the three-seat model was priced at $5,174. Production of both versions totaled 20,560.

In its second-to-last year of production, the 1991 Oldsmobile Custom Cruiser station wagon was totally redesigned and featured more rounded styling than the previous year's model. The three-seat wagon was priced at $20,495. It was powered by a 5.0-liter (307-cid) V-8. In a nod to the past, a "Vista" glass roof panel could be ordered. Anti-lock brakes were standard equipment.

Pontiac

The 1946 Pontiac Streamliner station wagon was offered in two versions: standard (with three seats) and Deluxe (with two seats), both having a wheelbase of 122 inches. This was the standard Streamliner, badged as having a straight-eight engine. Equipped with the straight eight, the wagon's price was $1,970. With the six-cylinder engine, the price was $28 less. The wood-bodied Pontiac wagons were built by the Ionia Body Co., and a fabric covered roof was used. Inside, imitation tan leather was featured.

In its second year of offering all-steel station wagons, Pontiac's 1950 Streamliner Deluxe wagon was available in both two- and three-seat configurations. The Silver Streak 8 script on the front fender signified that this Streamliner Deluxe was powered by a straight-eight engine. A six-cylinder version was also available. Pontiac also had a standard version of the Streamliner wagon, and both models used a two-piece tailgate. The six-cylinder Streamliner Deluxe was priced at $2,343 and the straight-eight version cost $2,411. The wagon's rear quarter windows featured sliding glass.

The Di-Noc exterior "wood" trim on this 1953 Pontiac Chieftain Deluxe station wagon was an $80 option. This wagon was powered by a straight-eight engine, but a six-cylinder powerplant was also offered. The Chieftain Deluxe wagon came with two seats and was priced at $2,590 with six-cylinder power and $2,664 with eight-cylinder power. This wagon's rear seat was the fold-down type and featured linoleum on its seat back. One of the interesting options that Pontiac offered in 1953 was the Auto-Home Remington electric shaver that plugged into the cigarette lighter.

In 1957, Pontiac's Safari name applied to all of its two- and four-door station wagons. This six-passenger Super Chief Deluxe Safari wagon featured Morrokide upholstery as standard and the whitewall tires and wire wheel covers were optional. All Safaris had V-8 power. Price of the Super Chief Deluxe Safari wagon was $3,021 and 14,095 were built.

Chevrolet had the Nomad and Pontiac offered this Star Chief Custom Safari two-door sport wagon in 1955, which was radically different from the wagons Pontiac had offered previously. This six-passenger Safari was powered by a V-8 and priced at $2,962. Production totaled 3,760. The roof panel and tailgate were shared pieces among the Nomad and Safari. This particular Safari was a prototype with an experimental two-tone roof.

The 1958 Pontiac Star Chief Custom Safari station wagon offered a roof rack, horizontal tailgate moldings and "Custom Safari" script on the tailgate as standard features. All Star Chiefs in 1958 had "stardust" carpeting. The Custom Safari wagon was powered by a V-8 engine. Price for the six-passenger wagon was $3,350 and 2,905 were produced. The Star Chief station wagon actually had a shorter wheelbase (122-inch) than the rest of the Star Chief line of cars (124-inch).

The 1960 Pontiac Catalina Safari station wagon was available in both two- and three-seat configurations. The V-8 engine was the rule for all Pontiacs. This (rear facing) three-seat version of the Catalina Safari featured a power-operated tailgate window, spare tire mounted under the cargo floor and Morrokide interior fabric. The rear quarter windows were of wraparound design. The fender-mounted antenna was a $30 option. Cost of the nine-passenger Catalina Safari wagon was $3,207 and 14,149 were built.

Both standard and Deluxe versions of the 1962 Pontiac Tempest Safari station wagon were available. This Deluxe model was a six-passenger wagon with a 112-inch wheelbase, and powered by an "Indy Four" four-cylinder engine. The Tempest Safari wagon featured a "hatchgate" rear door. The roof rack was a $65 option. Production total for the Deluxe wagon was 11,170.

The 1963 Pontiac Catalina Safari station wagon was available in six- and nine-passenger versions, with the former costing $3,171 and the latter priced at an additional $22. The two-tone paint was a $12.80 option. All Catalinas were powered by V-8 engines. Production of the two-seat wagon totaled 18,446 while the figure for the three-seat version was 11,751. A power-operated tailgate window was standard on the three-seat model.

The Pontiac Tempest Safari station wagon was introduced in 1967 as a one car, separate line. Simulated wood appliqué was standard. Cost of the six-passenger wagon was $2,936 and 4,511 were built. The OHC six-cylinder engine was standard, but this wagon was badged as having the optional high-performance four-barrel-carbureted 326-cid/285-hp V-8 with 10.5:1 compression.

In 1975, Pontiac's Grand Safari station wagon moved back to the Bonneville series from the discontinued Grand Ville series. Simulated wood appliqué was standard, but the luggage rack depicted was an $89 option. Base engine was the 400-cid V-8. The Grand Safari wagon was offered in both two- and three-seat versions with price being $5,433 and $5,580, respectively. Production figures were 2,568 and 4,752, respectively.

Depicted with optional $84 luggage rack, the 1970 Pontiac Executive Safari station wagon was offered in both six- and nine-passenger configurations. Simulated wood appliqué and full interior carpeting were standard. The two-seat Executive Safari cost $4,015 and 4,861 were built. Figures for the three-seat model were $4,160 and 5,629, respectively. Only V-8 power was available.

Pontiac's promotional copywriters came up with this bit to hawk the 1971 Grand Safari station wagon: "A fairy princess waving her magic wand isn't necessary to operate the new Glide-Away disappearing tailgate, standard on Pontiac's big station wagons for 1971...." The Grand Safari rode on a 127-inch wheelbase and was available in both six- and nine-passenger versions. Base engine was the 455-cid V-8. The second seat on both versions was the split-back-type. Price for the two-seater was $4,643 and production totaled 3,613. The three-seater's figures were $4,790 and 5,972, respectively.

The 1973 Pontiac LeMans Safari introduced the "hatchgate" rear door, which replaced the variable-opening tailgate used in previous years. The simulated wood appliqué and luggage rack depicted were part of the optional $317 Custom Safari package. Vent panes in the rear quarter windows were operational. Offered in both two- and three-seat versions, this three-seat LeMans Safari cost $3,547 and 6,127 were produced.

The 1988 Pontiac Safari station wagon was a (rear facing) three-seat model that sold for $14,519. A total of 6,397 were produced. Standard powerplant was the 5.0-liter (307-cid) V-8. Other standard features included: air conditioning, tinted glass, dual sport mirrors and tailgate window control. The Safari wagon rode on a 116-inch wheelbase. The simulated wood appliqué (above), wire wheel covers, luggage rack and rear window air deflector depicted were optional equipment.

Wagon Tales:
Cross-Country Sedan, Muddy Monster Chicken Wagon and Ole' Slurpy

Cross-Country Sedan

by Jimmy Davis
Wetumpka, Alabama

I was doing aircraft modifications at Air Force bases all over the country in 1958. Our 1956 Ford Victoria couldn't haul all of our belongings, so we traded it and $200 for a 1956 Ford Country Sedan four-door six-passenger station wagon. It had plenty of room for my wife, our seven-month-old daughter and me.

Everything we owned was carried with us in that wagon. My daughter ate many meals in her car seat as we traveled from airbase to airbase all over the country for the next two years. We had a place to put everything and it was loaded in the same spot each time we moved. The same boxes were always saved and used each time.

Thank heavens the wagon always got us there. Seldom did we ever have over $20 with us on trips. Gas was around 28 cents a gallon and motels were around four dollars a night for a decent one. Hamburgers were about 15 cents and we ate a lot of them! No credit cards in 1958; if things went wrong, you just waited until the next paycheck or borrowed the money from family or friends if you could.

We had a few problems with the wagon. Once when it was about 10 below zero in Rome, New York, the points closed. New ones were installed and the towing bill was six dollars. New U-joints in Kansas were $14. A new side window was about eight dollars in Kansas after I drove off without removing the drive-in speaker to beat the crowd out of the movie. I can still remember all of the amounts like it was yesterday. When you didn't have much money, each of these things that happened was a big deal. If an engine or transmission had gone out I still don't know what we would have done.

In 1963, I finally traded the trusty wagon for a 1960 Ford two-door sedan. Our daughter started crying at the dealership as they drove our wagon away. It was the only car she had ever known. If we had known how much trouble we would have with that sedan, I think my wife and I would have been crying with her. The 1956 wagon played a big part in our lives for five happy years when we were first starting our married life. Both of our daughters were born while we had it and I drove it to my first insurance job in 1960. I drove a 1956 Ford to work on July 8, 1996, when I retired from the insurance company. It also got me there and back that day as the wagon had 36 years before.

Jimmy Davis took this photograph of his wife and two-year-old daughter Kimberly posing with their 1956 Ford Country Sedan station wagon in 1959. In 1963, the wagon was traded in on a sedan that proved to be nowhere near as reliable as the Country Sedan.

Wagon production leaves 'em breathless

by Dr. Tom Johnson, M.D.
Williamston, Michigan

While in the Air Force serving as a physician during Vietnam, I was assigned to F.E. Warren Air Force Base in Cheyenne, Wyo. Traveling to northern Wyoming I happened upon a 1929 Model A Ford "woodie" in Kaycee, Wyo. I bought it, started to restore it and took it back to Michigan, where I began a pulmonary disease fellowship at the University of Michigan.

As part of my fellowship, I had the opportunity to attend the Tri-State Pulmonary Conference in Pembine, Wis. There I learned that, in 1929, because Ford had begun to mass produce station wagons in the Upper Peninsula, that a new disease had been described, and in fact, the man who had described it was at this conference. John Towey, M.D., during the 1920s and '30s was superintendent of the Pine Crest Sanitoria in Powers, Mich. Suddenly a number of men who worked at the Ford sawmill began to be admitted to the Sanitoria with possible tuberculosis. These men were short of breath and on x-ray were showing abnormalities on both sides of their lung fields. These abnormalities cleared rather rapidly without any treatment, and therefore, Dr. Towey knew it wasn't tuberculosis.

He visited the sawmill and found that during the sawing of the maple logs for station wagons there were great clouds of black dust in the air. He was told that these logs had been cut down a year or two earlier and were allowed to lie in the woods before being brought to the sawmill. He observed that men re-exposed to this black dust again developed the bilateral abnormalities on their chest x-rays along with the shortness of breath. By allowing the logs to lie in the woods, spores of a fungus had grown under the bark and when they were sawed the black dust in the air was these fungal spores. The men inhaled them and those who were susceptible developed an allergic reaction that created the abnormalities on the lung fields as well as the shortness of breath. Dr. Towey solved the problem by spraying water on the saw, which then kept the mold from going into the air. It worked fine.

In 1932, he wrote an article regarding this disease, which was published in *The Journal of the American Medical Association*. Maple bark disease was also known as Towey's Disease. It has only been described one time in print since then, occurring in a sawmill near Marshfield, Wis., in the 1960s.

Dr. Towey was elderly and a delightful man. I had the honor of presenting to him at the Tri-State Pulmonary Conference the next year, a piece of the original maple from my station wagon that I could not use, which I had had engraved into a nameplate for his desk. He died several years after this presentation.

A little known fact about the production of Model A Ford station wagons by Henry Ford in Michigan's Upper Peninsula is that a "new disease" was described because of it.

Cutting Edge Crosley

by Tom Kaiser
Sarasota, Florida

The following is a true story of my experience with a 1949 Crosley station wagon, then and now!

Back in the early 1950s, I used a 1949 Crosley station wagon in my insurance business in Cleveland, Ohio. I lived in an apartment building at the time, and every morning I would find the Crosley parked in the trash area so tight that it took me considerable time to "back-and-forth it" until I could get it out. It seems there were some practical jokers in the area who thought it was a panic to wedge the Crosley into the trash area.

One day, in desperation, I discussed this with the dealer from whom I bought the Crosley. He instructed me to drive the Crosley around to the body shop and he could solve that problem for me. I did as he instructed, and he got the body man to take his grinder and put an edge on the bottom of the bumpers at all four corners. After that was done, he told me I shouldn't have any more problems!

The next morning, I went to go to work, and lo and behold, there sat the Crosley right where I had parked it the night before! As I approached the car, however, I noticed some spots on the pavement. Further investigation revealed that there were four areas of blood stains just below the four corners of the bumpers! After that, I had *no* further problems with the Crosley being put in strange places. I can imagine the surprise of the practical jokers when they all four prepared to hoist up the Crosley that night, and all wound up with cut fingers! I imagine nowadays, one would be sued to high heaven for that!

That little Crosley served me well in the insurance business. When we would have a heavy snowstorm, I could be out adjusting claims when nothing else was moving. If the Crosley did become stuck, it was light enough that all I had to do was put it in first gear, open the door with the wheels slowly spinning, and give it a little boost, and off we would go as if nothing had happened!

Incidentally, Crosley was the first automaker with an all-steel station wagon, a 1948 model (introduced in late-1947)! Many people do not know that!

I had so many fond memories of that little wagon that in the mid-1970s I found one in Sarasota, restored it, and now have a ball running around in it! It is a car that was way ahead of its time.

Tom Kaiser's original 1949 Crosley station wagon, which had "cutting edge bumpers" to deter practical jokers who during the night liked to pick up the little wagon and move it.

Tom Kaiser's current 1951 Crosley station wagon, which he located in Florida and restored. This was the final year of manufacture for Crosley station wagons.

Speed Bump Sob Story

by F.L. "Pat" Jacobs
Snohomish, Washington

For many years while our children were small, we always had a station wagon, starting with a '57 Chevrolet 210 followed by a '60 Ford Ranch Wagon and finally a '67 Plymouth Belvedere.

The most memorable thing about the aforementioned station wagons was the experience in 1965, when we were spending a weekend in the mountains of Southern California, with three other couples. We were in a cabin near the village of Blue Jay. Somewhere on the western shore of Big Bear Lake, there was an exclusive new housing development underway. Upon completion it was to be gated with a guard and guardhouse at the entrance.

We decided to go visit this project, so seven of us got into the '60 Ford wagon. This was not a three-seater, but just a six-passenger model, so it was a little crowded--and as events would show, perhaps overloaded! We drove into the project, and drove around, admiring the lots to be, the views or lack thereof. On the way out, there was a speed bump, just short of the guardhouse. I slowed way down, and eased over, however, there was

a decided "bump" and then the screech of protesting metal. I slammed on the brakes, and jumped out expecting to find a mangled muffler. Worse! The gas tank was dragging on the ground, with only the fuel line holding it up!

Fortunately, I had a few tools, and the tank was about two-thirds empty. By lying on our backs, two of us could lift it back into place. I loosened the nuts on the J-bolts fastened to the straps, and with everyone straining we managed to get the retaining straps back in place. With the nuts re-tightened, we were on our way with dirtied clothes and aching muscles from the odd angle and the effort required.

Worse than that, however, was the soon-to-be-made discovery that the filler tube leaked with every right turn. Upon returning home, I took it to the local Ford dealer and a mechanic replaced an "O" ring that sealed the filler tube inside the inlet on the tank. The service manager listened to my sad story and then had the gall to say, "That's not so bad, I lost the gas tank on my Thunderbird on a freeway in the Bay area!"

Ole' "Slurpy"

by Doc Howell
Coeur d'Alene, Idaho

I've been hooked on station wagons for years, but was selective. I finally acquired a two-owner original 1975 Chrysler Town & Country wagon with 44,963 miles. My total investment was gas to drive it home to Idaho from Spokane, Wash., plus sales tax and license.

This Chrysler was ordered new by a Spokane dealer who put some 30,000 miles on it and then resold the wagon to an older couple. The dealer is also a Mopar hobbyist and had several nice cars stored in his Idaho summer home workshop, and had a desire to start winnowing down his inventory. The Town & Country was my "commission" for selling some cars from his storage facility. It seems the elderly couple he sold the wagon to experienced health problems and the husband had to be placed in a Spokane nursing home.

The Chrysler was stored outdoors and wasn't exactly as pictured at the time I acquired it. The hood cable was gone and the owner had punched a hole in the grille to accommodate a homemade hood release wire made from coat hangers. The hood also had a substantial depression aft of the hood ornament where someone had overexerted to get it closed. Fortunately, a cohort had a demolition derby Newport Custom parked conveniently in my backyard, which donated a cable and pristine hood. Another car donated a mint Newport Custom

grille. Eventually, this will all be replaced with a "long nose" '74 Imperial front header and bumper with waterfall grille and hidden headlamps; purists go away!

The Chrysler will definitely be a distinctive "media cruiser" when complete. My first efforts were naturally to get the wagon running properly after its long driveway sojourn. This included installing a 740 CFM Edelbrock electric choke carburetor and upgraded K & N air cleaner setup. Not a lightweight, this Chrysler, it earned the nickname "Slurpy" after the first two tanks of gas. With a 3.20:1 rear end ratio, I've decided to opt for either the #1406 Edelbrock carburetor or the 625 Carter since the purpose of the wagon is not to run races between stoplights.

The Town & Country's interior, moldings and glass were impeccable. It did require replacement of the rear dome light plate with switch, which was easily located in South Carolina. One missing door molding was located in Montana and the other in Ohio.

Apart from this trim, nothing cosmetic required immediate attention other than acquiring enough 3M Di-Noc faux vinyl woodgrain overlay to replace the existing "woodie" paneling.

I have heard umpteen horror stories about stripping cars with vinyl clad overlays such as this wagon. Every-

Due to its fuel consumption and riding characteristics, this 1975 Chrysler Town & Country is nicknamed both "Slurpy" and "Teddy" (Roosevelt of Rough Riders fame). The station wagon is owned by Doc Howell of Idaho.

thing from bead blasting to specially formulated aerosol sprays, etc. Nothing, though, produces results like elbow grease, a foot stool, a high-temperature heat gun and a putty knife honed to fine edge on the bench grinder.

The man who ordered the wagon said he kept the original window sticker and copy of his order (but not located as of this writing). I would definitely like to see the RPO list since this rig was ordered with the heavy-duty trailer towing package and has some unidentified electrical gear under the hood. The inner right front

fender has a short block mounted on it with a pair of what I call "screen door springs" that resemble the old "reverb radio units." Under the windshield washer reservoir is a finned unit that looks like part of an inverter setup or the block used for dual batteries.

I already have a set of air shocks for the rear along with a set of gas shocks for the front. The first time I crossed some railroad tracks with the Chrysler, I immediately changed its nickname from "Slurpy" to "Teddy" to commemorate the "Rough Riders!"

Del Rio Days

by Tom Turner
Orange, California

The first car I ever drove was a 1958 Ford Del Rio Ranch Wagon. I was but a wee lad when I went to my father (with quarters in hand from mowing lawns in the neighborhood) and said, "Dad, out of all the used cars we've looked at I like the '58 station wagon the best. Take this money and put it towards buying the wagon."

My dad did exactly that, and brought home the Ford station wagon the next day. There it was in all its glory with glistening chrome, shiny black and white paint, and a gorgeous red and white interior. The interior had that great new car smell, but back then it was from carpet and vinyl, not plastic like today's cars. Not long after

the homecoming of the majestic wagon we took it on the first of two vacations. We drove to Big Bear in the Southern California mountains, and I got to go fishing with my Dad.

The vacation went fine except for the trip home when we encountered one of those signs that reads "Falling Rock." This one meant business! Shortly after reading the sign, there was "Plymouth Rock" parked in the middle of our lane as we came around the curve. After careful consideration (?) my father decided to center the wagon over the rock and we would continue down the highway unscathed. As the wagon struck the boulder it gracefully went slightly airborne (or so it seemed) and with that, the center draglink, oil pan, transmission, bell housing and driveshaft were annihilated!

The driveshaft was bent so badly you could hear it (like thunder cracking) and feel the shaft crashing against the bottom of the car (like a bucking bronco), until we came to rest on the side of the road with oil, smoke and a trail of parts behind us. Shortly thereafter, the '58 was on the back of a tow truck and so was I, riding on a toolbox in front of the towing boom. I was staring at the front of the wagon mile after mile all the way home. It was the first time I felt sorry for the wagon.

After a few weeks the wagon was back on the road again just in time for my sister's first date, or some such event. Upon her coming home into the garage she misjudged the wall and knocked out the studs bringing the garage door down on top of the Ford and taking off all the side trim on the right side of the car. She continued to drive into the garage as though nothing had happened. Once again, I felt sorry for the wagon. The next day, my mother got into the wagon and was attempting to back out of the garage when a tire broke traction and began to spin because the car was wedged so hard against the wall. It was having a difficult time breaking free, but when it finally did it left the garage at a high rate of speed only to be stopped by the front end of my Dad's 1953 Ford Victoria. This time I felt sorry for the wagon and the Victoria. Obviously it wouldn't be just time and the elements that would lead to the demise of the wagon. My mother would play a large part in it too. For example, under the influence of alcohol, she would drive against the current of traffic miraculously not harming the wagon, but terrifying its occupants. How-

ever, she would later smash glass and cut up the padded dashboard and interior, leaving it in less than showroom condition.

After all was said and done, my father decided to sell the wagon to "One-eyed Jim" in 1969. Jim was a nice guy who was a customer on my paper route. This was great for me, as I could see the wagon every day as I passed by delivering my papers. Now, as I mentioned, Jim was a nice guy, but he, too, would lend a hand in the destruction of the wagon, as he had the use of only one eye! I felt sorry for Jim and the wagon. While passing the wagon every day I could get a damage report as I rode by. Looking at things such as heavy dents in the back bumper and a knocked-down pylon in the alley behind Jim's apartment, it was easy to tell what had happened given Jim's eyesight. Finally, when there wasn't a panel left to dent, a piece of chrome to bend, paint to scrape, or even a window to crack ... Jim moved away.

As the years passed, I thought of that wagon many times; how often I felt sorry for it, and about how awesome it might be to find one again and restore it. After a long six year search, which involved the placement of a few hopeful want ads, I located an advertisement in *Old Cars Weekly* that read "'58 For Sale." My wife and I were off to Grants Pass, Ore., from Orange County, Calif. There it was sitting under a canopy of pine trees. After some discussion (it was a rusted basketcase), we towed it home. Now, when I look at my wagon, I don't feel sorry for it, but for myself, when I think of all the countless hours of grueling work and thousands of dollars it will take to bring it back to life and be the kind of car I remember from my childhood.

We'll see ....

Bowties Are Always in Style

by Robert Vukas
Topeka, Kansas

I grew up in a Chevrolet station wagon family starting when dad brought me home from the hospital in a '54 210 Townsman, two-tone blue and white. My small hometown of Wayzata, Minn., had a family that needed our wagon for a wheelchair patient, so they contacted my dad. A deal was struck and our driveway had a new '57 210 Townsman, India ivory over Coronado yellow. The last memory I have of that car is of it going off to Village Chevrolet after reverse gear went out in it while rocking it in the snow of the winter of 1959-'60.

A new '60 Cascade green Parkwood wagon is the first car of which I have any vivid memories. Dad took what the dealer had that February, and it was equipped with a 348-cid V-8. He loved to challenge the early hot rods at intersections, who all gave him a funny look in that station wagon, but weren't laughing when he zoomed by. We truly saw the USA in our Chevrolet with a trip to Washington, D.C., and a trip around Lake Superior. In

the days before airbags and seatbelts, I spent a lot of time in the cargo area of that car.

Our last wagon was a '65 Bel Air. Dad bought it at the beginning of the model year and that was a mistake. The paint job was lousy and the leaf springs wore out tires quickly. The local dealer did fix the problems, though. We drove to Arizona in it and I remember the "cold" light below the dash. The one option worth noting was the electric rear window. The storage space below the cargo floor was nice, also. That Bel Air's 283-cid V-8 ran so smoothly it was almost silent.

Nineteen sixty-seven ushered in the era of Caprice sedans to our house. We never appreciated the hauling capacity of a station wagon more than when we did not have it. It would be another 22 years until my sister bought a '79 Impala that a member of our immediate family owned a wagon. That was followed up with an '84 Caprice. My brother got into the act with an '88 Celebrity. The closest I came to a new wagon-like vehicle would be my '82 Citation four-door hatchback.

Nineteen eighty-nine gave me my first true Chevrolet station wagon. While attending the Winfield, Kan., bluegrass festival, I saw a '57 Bel Air Townsman, two-tone India ivory over Colonial cream, which was almost an exact lookalike to my dad's car. I put my business card under the windshield wiper and wrote a note that read: "If you ever want to sell this car, please contact me." I received a letter four days later and by the following Sunday I was driving the car home.

I am the third owner of this car. The original owner had gone into a nursing home and the second owner purchased the car at his estate sale. The second owner had intended the car to be for his 12-year-old daughter

to use as a school car. She fell in love with a '66 Mustang convertible instead and as he was restoring a '59 Cadillac Eldorado at the time, he needed to sell the wagon to support the restoration of the other two.

Needless to say, I love station wagons for their utility and their style is also a plus. When I say my car can really haul, we're talking about groceries and cargo. I have restored the '57 to stock specifications except for the wide whitewall radial tires. I will not sacrifice handling, braking, and ride comfort. The fun is in the driving and there is nothing quite like seeing the dashboard lit up on the way home from a cruise, with the radio tuned to an oldies station.

As for my everyday car, I drive a 1991 Toyota Camry station wagon.

Honeymooning in a Land Yacht

by John Milliken, Jr.
Westlake Village, California

After completing my 1939 Cadillac convertible sedan restoration in 1985, I became interested in acquiring a wooden station wagon from the 1940s. I was pretty much confining my search to the more luxurious makes from General Motors--namely Buick or Pontiac--as I had always admired those body styles. A Packard from the 1948-'50 era hadn't crossed my mind--until I first saw one. I thought I had seen everything in the way of collectible cars during my 20-plus years of collecting and restoring them. But it was at the 1987 Barrett-Jackson auction in Scottsdale, Ariz., that I saw my first 1948 Packard "woodie"--or Station Sedan as Packard called it. This was a magnificent black, restored beauty. I liked everything about it--from its massive chrome front end

with its beautiful cormorant hood ornament resting on top of a rounded hood, flowing into broad front fenders, to its sweeping barrel-back tailgate section. I had to find one like this to restore.

A month after the auction, I was on a layover in Minneapolis with my job as a pilot for Delta Airlines. While reading *Hemmings Motor News* in my hotel room that day I came across an ad for, you guessed it, a 1948 Packard "woodie"--and it was right there in Minneapolis. Having a few hours to kill before my next flight, I called the owner. He picked me up, I drove the car, and, in what turned out to be too hasty a decision, I made an offer and bought the car. A week later, on Feb. 28, 1987, I married Leslie. The next day, we flew to Minneapolis to

"A virtual land yacht in the truest sense of the word" is how John Milliken describes his maroon 1948 Packard Station Sedan. It took him three-plus years to restore the "woodie".

pick up our "honeymoon car" and spent the next five days leisurely driving it back to our home in Sacramento. Except for a fuel pump leak in Wyoming, for which I had brought a spare (the only spare I brought with me so I must have ESP), the car performed flawlessly.

It was only after I got the car home and began to dismantle it for restoration that I realized that I had been too hasty in my decision to buy it. What I saw and bought was a complete car, with good wood and interior, that had new tires and ran well. Yes, there was visible rust--the floors and rocker panel, typical of a car that began its life in Montana, then spent its days in Minnesota prior to my "rescuing" it.

Still, I thought it was worth saving. But it was not until I cut out the floor and rocker panels that I realized that this was going to be the challenging, extensive and expensive restoration that it became. Beneath the rusted floors, the eight large brackets that connect the body to the frame rails were all rusted through so badly that, had I hit a deep pothole, I might well have ended up with the entire body sitting on the ground. There was no question now that the body would have to come off the frame. My at-home restoration now became a professional body-off restoration that would consume the next three years of work, plus a couple of more years to pay off the home equity loan to finish the job.

After completely dismantling the car at home and having it sandblasted, I carted it off to Ed Cook, pro-

prietor of Classic Productions, a Sacramento restoration shop that specializes in Thunderbirds and Mustangs. There he employed an old Frenchman and master body builder named Guy. I was amazed at watching this craftsman at his work. Over the next

1948 Packard Station Sedan - Series 2293

Price when new: $3,425
Engine: L-Head straight eight
Bore and stroke 3.5 x 3.75 inches
130 horsepower
7.0:1 compression ratio
Differential: 4.10:1
Transmission: three-speed with overdrive
Wheelbase: 120 inches
Weight: 4,075 pounds
Options: radio, heater, power antenna, visor, overdrive, fog lamps, backup light, dual spotlights, cormorant, whitewalls

The cargo area of John Milliken's restored 1948 Packard Station Sedan.

few months he virtually recreated the lower body on my car exactly as Packard made it, and in some ways even better, for he made a few changes to factory "pockets" that retained water, which could lead to rust. And not one speck of body filler or lead had to be used. I was quite pleased despite spending nearly $13,000 just for the body work.

Ed Cook was kind enough to let me work in his shop on days off during the next couple of years. The honeymoon car almost became the divorce car, however, as we moved to Lake Oswego, Ore., in 1988, about one-and-a-half years before I completed the restoration. My wife saw little of me because I spent most of my days in Sacramento. A Christmas present to her of custom license plate frames reading "Leslie's 1948 Packard Woodie" only appeased her for a few months.

I did about 60 percent of the restoration work myself: mainly research, dismantling, finding parts, putting together, carting things off to be woodgrained, refinished or plated, minor mechanical work and, in general, spearheading the operation. Classic Productions handled the body work, painting, interior and wiring. The engine, despite getting us to Sacramento from Minneapolis, was shot and required a total rebuild (with hardened valves and valve seats to allow the burning of unleaded gas) as did the overdrive and suspension.

Gauges, radio and clock were also rebuilt. I purchased aftermarket dual spotlights and side rearview mirrors and, from a want ad in *Hemmings*, found magnificent new old stock fog lamps, backup light (in original Packard boxes) and accessory day/night mirror with amber glass. I also rebuilt my vacuum antenna, which works fine. The wood is original but nicely refinished.

Well, my project (nightmare?) was finally complete on May 5, 1990--three years and two months after I started it. And it turned out magnificent; that blonde northern birch wood with mahogany inserts set against a Cavalier maroon paint scheme, lots of chrome and saddle vinyl upholstery makes this a virtual land yacht in the truest sense of the word.

In addition to looking great, the car drives like a dream. There were about 1,800 of these Station Sedans built by Packard in 1948 and just over 3,000 in the 1948-'50 period. They were basically identical except for minor front bumper and trim changes.

You have the best of everything in the 1948 Packard Station Sedan: the luxury of all-vinyl interior, door panels and headliner, the rigidity and quietness of an all-steel body, the beautiful appearance of a wooden body and the practicality of a station wagon. It is easy to see why this luxurious wagon was popular with the country club set of its day.

Government Surplus Station Wagon

by Gary Schwertley
Edmonds, Washington

While on active duty during the Vietnam war, I discovered that the Army PX sold new cars and arranged delivery back in the United States when the buyer returned home. I picked up a sales brochure for the 1971 full-size Ford line and decided I would look into buying one when it was time to go home. By the time I was to go home, it was 1972. In the urgency to get out of Vietnam and get home, I forgot about the new car.

A few years later, in 1975, I was working at the headquarters of an Infantry division. For the use of the division staff, we had five 1972 Ford Custom sedans and several 1971 Ford Custom sedans. I got to drive the 1972 Ford sedans quite a lot and really liked them, sometimes saying to myself, "I should have gone ahead and bought one of these while I was in Vietnam." I left the division headquarters and the Fords in 1977 and forgot about them.

Many years later, I noticed a couple of 1972 Fords being auctioned as surplus U.S. Government property in a GSA auction list. One was a former U.S. Army sedan, on which I missed the bid. The other was a former U.S. Air Force Custom 500 station wagon, on which I was the successful bidder.

I got the U.S. Air Force station wagon in 1993, so after 21 years of government use it needed some repairs, which I did. The car is an eight-passenger station wagon and is equipped with Ford's 351 Cleveland engine with two-barrel carburetor and FMX automatic transmission.

I told my wife, "I finally got hold of my favorite car after all these years and it is a station wagon to boot." Of the government-purchased 1971 and 1972 Fords, station wagons were rather rare. The government had to pay a few bucks extra for the Custom 500 in the station wagon models, as the base Custom Ranch Wagon did not come with the extra two seats under the rear decking. Government sedans were Custom models.

My Ford's Air Force service was spent mainly with the 62nd Airlift Wing at McChord AFB, Wash. It was also used at an Air Force facility at Grant County Airport in Moses Lake, Wash., where it was used on the runway with red light bar and siren equipment.

Since 1993, I was lucky enough to find a nice 1972 Ford Custom 500 sedan--sort of a companion car to the station wagon. This car is unique in that it was manufactured with the Ford 302-cid V-8 engine, which was unusual in 1972. Of the few made, fleet sales accounted for their disposition. Because it was sold so late in the year (December 1972), I suspect that it was built for fleet sales but washed out for some reason and was spun off to a dealer to sell at a discount to a private buyer. It was an old man's car, and an old man bought it, preserving it for over 20 years so I could have it!

Gary Schwertley's 1972 Ford Custom 500 Ranch Wagon, a former U.S. Air Force vehicle. He purchased the Ford at a government surplus auction after 21 years of trying to acquire his favorite car.

Aged Wood

by Coy Thomas
Port Angeles, Washington

Every town has a legendary old car that people in that area either remember or know about presently. Such a car still exists in Port Angeles, Wash.

However, to fully appreciate this story, we must travel back to 1946. That's when John Wagner got out of the Coast Guard and headed directly to the Samuelson Motor Co. Ford dealership in Port Angeles to order a new 1947 Ford "woodie" wagon. At the same time, Wagner's good friend, Harry Schoffel of the famous Olympic Hot Springs, also ordered a new 1947 Ford "woodie" from the same dealership.

When Wagner's maroon-fendered wagon arrived, his friend needed a car immediately for his lodge business. Wagner, being a good acquaintance and understanding of his friend's dilemma, graciously allowed his new maroon wagon to go to his close friend. Wagner waited a few additional weeks for the next shipment of '47 Fords to arrive at the dealership. Within a short period of time, the Ford dealership called Wagner and announced that his new gray-fendered "woodie" had arrived. At that time, the wagon's future started to unfurl.

Wagner and his wife, Dode, had already started their family and business in town. The gray "woodie" was a daily driver family car for many years to follow. During these many years, the '47 wagon carried supplies to the Wagner's diner, gas and grocery store. In addition to these chores, the Ford also ran errands that four children Bonnie, John Jr., Gary and Teresa required.

Wagner is an avid outdoorsman and with a love for hunting and fishing in the great northwest, he instilled in his children the love for our environment through family campouts. His son, John Jr., admits that some of his fondest childhood memories were of camping outdoors and sleeping in the wagon on overnight treks.

By 1968-'69, after forging streams and jumping stumps over the 70 acres at Little River and all of the Olympic Peninsula, the Ford was showing signs of wear and tear. The Wagner family decided to have the fenders repainted gray, a new top installed, and a rebuilt flathead engine installed to gain additional years of service. The "woodie" was now notorious as "Wagner's Woodie" and it had become a well-known sight around Port Angeles. By now, it was used as a second car for the Wagner family.

As 1974 approached, the Ford received its final current license renewal tag and was maintained occasionally until January 1997. At that time, the Wagner family agreed, after owning the Ford for 50 years, that they would sell it to a Port Angeles old car enthusiast.

The '47 "woodie" found an excellent home 50 years ago and it will now remain in Port Angeles—and not be "the one that got away!"

John Wagner purchased this 1947 Ford "woodie" new from Samuelson Motor Co. of Port Angeles, Washington.

"Wagner's Woodie" is the nickname for this 1947 Ford station wagon, owned for 50 years by John Wagner of Washington state. It is a well-known old car in the Northwest.

Wood is Good!

by Tom Minor
Andover, Minnesota

Having grown up around both Chrysler products and a Dad who is a carpenter, it was only natural that it was "love at first sight" when I spotted the old 1949 Plymouth "woodie" wagon parked on a side street in Siren, Wisconsin. A friend and I were on a salvage yard safari, looking for parts for the old Plymouths that we were each trying to fix on minimal budgets. It was 1972, and I had been married just a few months earlier and was still trying to convince my new bride that old cars were something special (something that after 25 years, I'm still not sure I've succeeded in doing!).

We drove around the block to get a better look at the Plymouth and were pleasantly surprised to see a faded "For Sale" sign in the window. I could only speculate that the sign must have graced the windshield of some other vehicle and that would account for its sorry state because certainly a Plymouth wagon would have sold immediately! Nobody was home so I copied the phone number and called later in the evening after returning home (approximately 100 miles away). I discovered that not only was the old Plymouth for sale but that at $250, it was even within my budget! And, best of all, it actually was driveable! This latter point may be lost on many people, but considering some of the other "dreams" I had purchased up to this point, anything even moveable was something to celebrate.

Arrangements were made to pick up the old Plymouth. With its classic wood sides I was sure that my wife would fall in love with it. To make it even more attractive, I decided I should probably pick it up with a friend and spend some time working on it over at my folk's house and put in a new floor. (Just a guess, but I suspected that the gaping hole where a passenger's feet would rest would have an immediate and adverse effect on my wife's feelings toward the car.)

After a hardy day's work with a torch and some sheet metal, the old Plymouth was ready for my wife. It's hard to believe, but she didn't seem as enthused about the car as I was! She made some reference to the fact that as long as she did not have to be seen in it, she didn't care what I drove. She also let me know that it would be best if I could find some place to park it other than right below the living room window of the apartment that we were renting. That way, hopefully, nobody would identify her with the car.

The Plymouth proved itself amazingly dependable throughout the fall. I parked it for the winter and started driving it again the next summer. I was even able to convince my wife that it had some practical merit for hauling, since it did have a lot of room in back. We even drove it to an old car show in Grand Rapids, Minn., that summer -- a trip that it made without any problems whatsoever. For the show, I spent a whole afternoon sanding down the wood and applying a new coat of varnish. You just cannot be too careful with a desirable collectible like that Plymouth! I even went as far as stuffing wood filler into some of the larger cracks. It didn't really look too bad when I was done (from 100 feet away!).

The next winter we did not have the luxury of two "regular" cars, so I decided to drive the old Plymouth. Once again, I was surprised at its dependability. It started every day and could go through an amazing amount of snow without becoming stuck. These were the years that studded snow tires were still legal and I supposed this helped a lot, too. One of my most memorable times with the car that winter was when I decided to skip work for a day and drive to Hutchinson, Minn., to look through a small salvage yard. I was going a bit too fast on one corner that was icy and went off the road. Thinking that the best thing to do was to accelerate and try to get back up on the road, I stepped it down hard. The result was that I went even further off the road before coming to a complete stop. This didn't seem too bad so I got out the jack and a shovel, thinking that I would raise the car, dig the snow out from under, clear a path to the highway, and drive out.

The first inkling I had that this plan was not going too well was when the jack went its full height without even hitting the ground, and the Plymouth had not raised an inch. Well, it looked as if a tow was in order! What a disgrace.

I walked up the road to the nearest farm, knocked on the front door, and asked if it was possible to get some help. At first the guy wasn't all that eager to help, but eventually reluctantly agreed to help. He went out to a shed, grabbed a bunch of chain, got his big old John Deere tractor started, and headed out to the road. He did get a bit friendlier when he saw the Plymouth -- he must have really liked it because he started smiling. In fact, his smile soon turned into laughter -- I guess he loved it! He had a hard time hooking up the chain, laughing as he was. He just had to tell me about the last "kid from the city" that he had rescued – it seems that my predecessor had driven his car into a small river while looking for a good place to park for a while with his girlfriend. I did not see the connection, but since he was having fun, it was fine with me! He did get the car out just fine and wouldn't even accept any payment. He said the entertainment value was worth every minute of it!

Later in the winter, while on a grocery run, the old Plymouth died in the middle of a busy intersection and we had to push it out of the way (at -25 degrees!). This put my wife in a lousy mood towards the Plymouth, so once it was running again I just parked it for a few weeks to let the whole episode age a bit. Before driving it again that winter I even bought some cheap weatherstripping and glued it around the doors. My wife just didn't like the way the snow and cold air blew in her face when we were driving. She thought this was a nice improvement, but also mentioned that it would be nice if it had a heater. It had one, but it was no match for the incoming drafts. So, to remedy this situation, I taped clear plastic as a divider behind the front seat and added another heater (dual heat!), suspended beneath the dash by some re-twisted coat hangers. I thought it was really nice now, but it seemed as if we took the other car most of the time anyway.

The following spring we purchased our first home. Moving day was really neat -- we put the old Plymouth to full use. I took out the extra seats and made a bunch of trips loaded with boxes and furniture. Needing some help, I asked my brother if he had some time, so he showed up with his 1947 Dodge pickup and attached trailer made from an old truck box. While our moving vehicles maybe did not look real professional, they did the job just fine. All day long the neighbors across the street kept looking at us; I never could figure out just what they were staring at!

The following summer the well went dry at the same time the savings account also went dry. Family assets were minimal, we didn't want to take out a loan, and the old Plymouth had become a fixture under a tarp behind the garage. So, I cleaned it up and advertised it for $750, thinking that nobody would pay this much, but my good wife would at least think I was trying to be practical. Unfortunately, some guy showed up with cash and drove away in the Plymouth. It made me sad to see it driving away, but I kept his name and phone number and figured that down the road I would be able to buy it back. This never happened, of course, and I went on to own several other old Plymouths that were down on their luck.

A number of years later I met someone who mentioned he had once seen an old Plymouth wagon like mine, rusting out in a woods, with a big oak tree lying across it. Since this was in the same area that the Plymouth's new owner lived, I presumed that was the end of it. I never really knew if this was the case, and the thought makes me feel bad because it would have been nice to see it restored. However, maybe this was a fitting end to an old Plymouth "woodie"!

Cool Runner

This modified 1961 Dodge Pioneer station wagon is owned by Steve Drahos of Atlanta, Georgia. It is the nine-passenger model with a 318-cid V-8 engine and air conditioning (which is in the process of being rebuilt).

Vending Machine

by Alfred Orzechowski
Somerdale, New Jersey

I am 67 years old. I have owned a 1955 Chevrolet Bel Air station wagon since April 1974.

I am retired from New Jersey Bell Telephone (now Bell Atlantic of New Jersey). I put in 37 years there. The way I found this wagon was because of my job. My Bel Air is a four-door model painted Gypsy red and Shore-line Beige. Mack, a friend of mine at work, told me where it was. I, myself, had seen it on occasion being driven by a woman. Some time had passed, and it just seemed to have vanished.

Mack told me it was parked behind a house and it didn't have any tags on it. Well, that made it interesting to me. I drove over to the address and spoke to the lady who owned it. The wagon belonged to her father, who was the

original owner. That evening, I phoned her and spoke with her husband. The price for the Bel Air was $500.

I went over the following Saturday, put tags on it, and drove it home. That was April 1974. I drove the wagon as daily transportation until 1979. When the transmission quit, I had both the engine and transmission overhauled. From that time on, it was registered antique. Now, I only drive it sparingly.

I use the 1955 station wagon to vend out of at Carlisle, Pa. I am one of the original 200 vendors at that show. I am the only vendor there with the same vehicle for over 20 years.

Over the years, many people have wanted to buy my Chevy; however, it is not for sale -- at least not now.

Alfred Orzechowski's 1955 Chevrolet Bel Air station wagon, which he has used to vend from at the Carlisle, Pa., old car shows for over 20 years.

146

Converted Cadillac

by Burton Park
Tiffin, Ohio

My 1978 Cadillac Fleetwood Brougham was converted from a four-door sedan to a station wagon for the original owner at a cost approaching the price of the new Cadillac Fleetwood sedan from which it was built. The conversion took six weeks and was accomplished by using a General Motors wagon roof, tailgate, luggage rack and third rear-facing seat. It also has a full red leather interior, AM-FM-CB radio, rear self-leveling suspension, four wheel disc brakes and, of course, air conditioning, power steering and brakes.

I have driven station wagons as my daily transportation for 35 years because of their ability to provide adequate hauling capacity while maintaining a big car ride. In the past, I have owned Oldsmobiles, Buicks, Pontiacs and a Suburban, so I just could not pass up an opportunity to have a Cadillac station wagon.

Burton Park's 1978 Cadillac Fleetwood Brougham station wagon conversion. Note that the tailgate swings open or drops down.

www.wagon master

by Steve Manning
Darnestown, Maryland

I have been a station wagon lover for as long as I remember...

I learned to drive in a 1963 Ford Fairlane 500 wagon. I now own (and am in the process of restoring) the only station wagon my parents bought new -- a highly-optioned, big-block 1968 Plymouth Sport Suburban. I still remember driving home from the dealership in that car (I was about 10 years old). I have all the documentation and service records, including documentation of the time my father sued Chrysler when they did not fix things to his satisfaction.

My daily driver is another station wagon, a 1990 Audi 200 turbo quattro, which among other modifications now produces 300 hp (and has brakes to match).

I am the owner of the Internet domain, www.station-wagon.com (see related story in this book, which includes a photo of Mr. Manning's Plymouth). It is dedicated to station wagons and I encourage all car enthusiasts to take a look! I've been working on it since mid-1997 and have a good start.

Georgia Peach

by Michael Pearson
Brookfield, Connecticut

Although my first "old car" was a 1958 Edsel Citation two-door hardtop that I bought in 1992 (and which I still own), I've always had a longing for an older station wagon for several reasons. First, as a kid growing up in the late 1950s and '60s, I can remember riding in many different station wagons although my parents never owned one. I can still remember my favorite being a 1967 Chevrolet Caprice nine-passenger wagon that one of my friend's parents owned. Just to sit in the rear-facing third seat was a real treat.

With the growing popularity of sport utilities and minivans, I guess the increasing rarity of station wagons is another reason why I've wanted to own one. I imagine most wagons lived a good life of 10-15 years of hauling kids and cargo and then ended up at the crusher. Consequently, it's still unusual to spot older wagons on the road.

In the spring of 1994 a friend of mine in Atlanta who knew I was interested in a wagon forwarded me a local *Auto Trader* that had a photo ad of an old 1959 Plymouth station wagon, and he promised to check it out. Within weeks, I arranged to have a friend fly down to Atlanta to pick up the car. Even though it hadn't been regularly driven since 1967, it didn't take much to get the car roadworthy and licensed.

William Johnson of Kingsport, Tennessee, had been the wagon's original owner and had purchased the car in the spring of 1959 from a Plymouth dealership in Church Hill, Tennessee. At the time, Johnson continued to drive his 1953 Dodge four-door sedan.

The glovebox was full of old insurance papers, oil change receipts, and old gas station maps of the southeastern United States. From some of the insurance papers, it appeared that Johnson had seen a career change sometime in the late 1950s from "janitor" to "funeral home director." (As late as 1996, the Kingsport, Tennessee-based insurance company still existed -- and even had employees who remembered Johnson and his Plymouth wagon!)

Johnson and his wife eventually retired to Eatonton, Georgia, in the mid-1960s, and after both passed away, the wagon apparently ended up with a daughter around 1967. Her family found the car "too ugly to drive" and the car was parked under some pine trees around 1972. With only 29,216 original miles, it was left at the mercy of neighborhood kids who, by the looks of the station wagon when purchased, must have used it for target practice with rocks and baseball bats.

Surprisingly, the Plymouth required very little to make it roadworthy (a testament, I guess, to the reliability of the 318-cid engine). New hoses, spark plugs, and a fuel pump and it was ready to go. Nevertheless, my friend who picked up the car had to put blankets on the front seats since the interior had completely rotted out after sitting for so many years in the hot Georgia sun.

Before departing Atlanta, my friend said farewell to several local friends by taking them in the Plymouth to an outdoor Mexican restaurant. As the restaurant patrons stared at the sight of five people getting out of this weary old wagon, various stainless steel side trim fell off both sides of the wagon as all four doors were slammed by the exiting passengers. Fortunately, it was all recovered and placed in the back cargo area.

The 22-hour trip from Georgia to Connecticut was accomplished with little incident, although it was soon discovered that this trip had been made with two broken push rods -- not to mention the increasing sight of smoke belching from the Plymouth's tailpipe.

Using my subscriptions to *Old Cars Weekly* and *Hemmings Motor News*, I quickly went to work trying to find

Michael Pearson, relaxing in the back seat, drove his 1959 Plymouth Custom Suburban from Connecticut to the American Station Wagon Owners Association show in Indianapolis in 1997. The year before, Pearson traveled to California in the car, including some of Route 66 when returning to Connecticut.

trim parts, interior needs, and on and on. Many of these items have interesting stories of their own. For instance, I found aluminum insert trim for the side of the wagon on a 1959 Belvedere four-door sedan I spotted in a salvage yard near Waterbury, Connecticut. (And while there, I discovered many other '59 Plymouth wagons I could turn to for parts.) After balking at a price of $130 per taillight to have the housings rechromed, I soon found new old stock (NOS) taillights in their original boxes for $40 for the pair. The "swamp cooler" air fan came from a friend's 1958 Edsel Corsair. The luggage rack came from a 1963 Plymouth in an Arizona salvage yard. The white and gold rear, car-width mudflap came from a guy in Illinois whose father used to own a Western Auto store -- the original box still showed the address as "Chicago 7, Illinois." A new original front bumper came from a Chrysler-Plymouth dealer in Sheridan, Wyoming. The stories are endless.

Although it continues to be an "ongoing project," the Plymouth reached a stage in late 1995 where I knew it was reliable enough to drive long distances to car shows. So, in early 1996, I began planning a trip that would take me across the United States that I knew

would fulfill a lifetime wish -- and a trip I knew I would probably never repeat.

By taking three weeks of vacation and coordinating my agenda so I could attend several car shows en route, I planned to drive from Connecticut to Denver to San Luis Obispo, California. I would then return by the southern route so I could travel some sections of old Route 66.

What was totally unexpected was that at every gas station, rest stop, restaurant and motel, I always seemed to run into people who had owned a station wagon at one time or even a '59 Plymouth wagon in particular. This alone was worth the trip.

The first problem I encountered was related to high altitude driving. I almost didn't make it through Eisenhower Pass on I-70 in Colorado. With a little tinkering of the timing and removing the air cleaner, I finally made it to the other side of the pass. The next incident occurred about 65 miles into a 120-mile stretch in southern Utah where there were posted warnings of "no services" during those 120 miles. A tire blew. Although I easily replaced it with a spare, I didn't feel too comfortable not having a spare until I reached California.

Because of several stops to visit salvage yards, I timed my desert segment to Las Vegas rather poorly and drove the stretch of I-15 south of Cedar City, Utah, after 3:00 in the afternoon. Yes, it was hot!

Although I later made it through Los Angeles traffic without incident, my generator light went on near Santa Monica. As I limped into a McDonald's parking lot, I soon discovered that my generator had completely burnt up. Fortunately, a gentleman in the parking lot noticed my dilemma, mentioned a repair shop nearby, and by 6:00 p.m., I was on the road again. (Ironically, the good Samaritan who helped had just moved to the area from Connecticut and, in fact, had once lived about one mile from my house!)

Because I was short on time, I didn't get to drive as much of Route 66 that I would have liked; this certainly would have been the perfect car to travel on some of those old stretches. Of particular interest were the 1940s and 1950s-era motels in Tucumcari, New Mexico. And, after returning to Connecticut, I was already planning my trips for 1997.

In addition to attending my first American Station Wagon Owners Association show in Indianapolis, I also had two other firsts in 1997. I attended my first Plymouth Club show (in Kansas City) and my first trip to Iola, Wisconsin. At the Plymouth show, I was shocked to be not only the only 1959 vehicle in attendance, but the only station wagon as well.

My Plymouth station wagon had been built in Detroit on February 17, 1959, and was one of 35,024 six-passenger Custom Suburbans built for 1959. (It had sold for a base price of $2,881 in 1959, and the Custom Suburban was actually the mid-trim line of the three series of station wagons that Plymouth offered that year.)

Out of curiosity, I had an information service check all 50 states' Department of Motor Vehicle offices to see how many '59 Plymouth Custom Suburban wagons were still registered. Surprisingly, as of mid-1997, there were only 117 still registered for road use. Fortunately, most of the salvage yards I've visited across the United States seem to have one or two of these wagons, so I don't think the 117 of us still driving them are going to be hurting for parts anytime soon.

Bonneville Come Back!

by Rodger Airey
Marlton, New Jersey

As my son enters his Junior year of high school, his interest in cars has become somewhat of an obsession. It is not his fault. He comes by it honestly. Heck, I still have all my Tootsietoys, slot cars and models from the 1950s and '60s.

What I do not have, though, is my first real car, a 1960 Pontiac Bonneville Safari. At the time, I guess it may not have been that special. A station wagon was not what I had in mind. My dad bought it for me for $125 in the spring of 1969. It had 125,000 miles on it, but it was pretty clean. It enabled me to get to my part-time job in the summer, and I could fill it up with friends and tire tubes for daily trips to the lake.

My parents were pretty cool when it came to cars. My dad was and remains an avid race car fan. He was president of his sports car club and my parents brought home a lot of trophies after taking their '65 Mustang GT fastback on rallies. Later they traded it in on a beautiful Calypso Coral '70 Mustang Mach 1. I was always eager to borrow their Mustang.

My Pontiac never gave me much trouble except during the winter that the transmission started slipping. It ran pretty well but the transmission was steadily getting worse. I do not recall exactly what the mechanic said, but it had something to do with the clutches. Anyway, about March, when things tended to thaw out during the day and refreeze at night, my wagon became frozen in a muddy area of the driveway and I could not break it free in the morning before school.

I pointed out the necessity to my mom of borrowing the Mach 1. Of course, this looked like a ploy to show off at school, hence her refusal. I subsequently got back in the wagon, revved up its 389-cid V-8 and dropped it in gear. My friends said they could hear my engine explode from a block away. My dad paid $10 to have the car towed away. With a bad transmission and a blown engine, there was no way to justify the repairs. The $150 replacement Ford Falcon was more than sufficient to get me around for a couple of years. About a week later, one of my buddies let me know that my Bonneville had arrived at the junkyard he worked in and it was crushed.

I have been involved with cars ever since in one way or another. Oddly, it never occurred to me until recently that I always tended to gravitate toward the station wagons at shows and car corrals. That first car left me with a permanent fondness for station wagons. I don't know if I will ever find a decent, fairly-priced one like it again. I have never seen another on the road, probably because only 5,163 were ever made. I spotted a few wrecks in salvage yards and a couple for sale in national publications, but these were out of my price range. If only I had known then what I know today!

Well, at least I can impress upon my son to learn a lesson from my story. He and I have been working together and enjoying a '70 Pontiac LeMans Sport. This candy apple red beauty is a keeper and I really think he understands what he's got. There is nothing like your first car and it can never be replaced.

Heading for Adventure

Greg Knoll of Oak Harbor, Washington, is the boy pictured at the far right in this 1968 photo. His family is loaded and ready to move from Long Beach, Calif., to Oak Harbor, Wash. The car is a 1963 Ford Country Sedan.

Now the year is 1997. The boys in Pontiac station wagon are Greg and Peggy Knoll's sons, Garrett and Jason Knoll. The car is a 1965 Pontiac Catalina Safari. Greg Knoll said, "Now we load up our gear and boys in our station wagon and head for adventure. Our Pontiac was purchased from the original owners in the spring of 1997. It's a nice original car."

1972 Ford "Concertmobile"

by Steve Walker
Waterloo, Iowa

When I was growing up in the 1960s, we were one of the few families that did not have a station wagon. So this is not a story of growing up as a kid traveling across America in the family station wagon.

I first was introduced to station wagons a bit later in life. The year was 1974. I was 19 years old and a freshman at Iowa University. My best friend and high school buddy Dave also attended college with me. We were roommates.

Dave's father happened to be a traveling salesman who owned a 1972 Ford Country Squire, so take a wild guess which car Dave got to use for college? His Dad's station wagon. At this time, I thought that wagons might be okay for someone who had a family -- but they were definitely not cool to be seen in around campus. We were a bunch of long-haired hippies and driving the old man's car didn't quite fit our rebellious image.

All that would soon change, though. Nineteen seventy-four was a big year for rock concerts. It seemed as if every major band was out on tour. Crosby, Stills, Nash & Young just happened to be playing in St. Paul, so we decided to hop in the wagon and head north for Minnesota. It didn't take long for me to change my opinion of the lowly station wagon. Keep in mind, I was used to driving a plain Jane '63 Ford.

This station wagon was loaded! First, it was huge--we had plenty of room. It had power steering and brakes, electric seats and windows, cruise control and air conditioning. It also had a great stereo system. It's like, what more could we ask for in a car? So we packed the cooler, placed it on the back seat, and away we went. We were traveling in comfort and in style. It didn't take me long cruisin' down the road to think to myself, "Man, this is the only way to go!"

We partied for several hours all the way to St. Paul, saw a great concert and then started back towards home. By this time, we were pretty wasted and knew that there was no way we could make it back home. So guess what we did? We pulled off the interstate, found the first gravel road and took it until we found a farm field entrance. We backed the wagon in and shut it off. Then we folded down the back seat and had the perfect place to crash for the night. We woke up the next morning and were on the road again. From that point on, I became an avid station wagon fan.

It never really mattered to me what people thought about my long hair, so needless to say, it also didn't matter what they thought about station wagons. We knew the truth ... it was the perfect "concertmobile." And I've been driving one ever since.

I now own the following station wagons: a 1966 Ford Ranch Wagon, which received the "Best Daily Driver" award at the 1997 American Station Wagon Owners Association convention and a 1985 Pontiac Parisienne Safari Wagon--the best station wagon I have ever owned.

Brotherly Love of Wagons

by Keith Gumbinger
Kenosha, Wisconsin

My wife Carol and I own a '49 Ford "woodie" wagon. It has special meaning for us since my parents also owned a '49 Ford "woodie" when I was in grade school. My Dad would often take us kids to school in it and I would usually sit in the third seat way in the back. Despite what the Ford sales brochures state, the third seat was really only suitable for kids or smaller adults since it is positioned on top of the rear axle hump and does not offer much leg room between it and the middle seat.

Our Ford and the one my parents had are identical except for their colors. Our's is Seamist green, while their's was maroon. Both have the 100-hp flathead V-8 and standard shift. The '49s were Ford's first all-new body style after the war. These cars are significant in that the wood was ornamental and not structural as on the '48s and earlier.

We take the "woodie" to the Iola (Wisconsin) Old Car Show every year and display it in the event's Blue Ribbon area. We obtained many parts for this car at the Iola meet and through Old Cars Weekly. The maple on the wood panels is original, but the mahogany is new. My wife refinished the wood, painted the car and did much of the assembly. The headliner is from Dennis and Kathy Bickford of Vintage Woodworks in Iola. Dennis and my wife teamed up to install the headliner.

My brother, John, also drives a station wagon, a 1966 AMC Rambler Classic 770 station wagon. He and his wife, Pauline, live in Lake Stevens, Wash. John was also born and raised in Kenosha and has always liked AMC products. After their marriage, he and Pauline moved to Washington and he got a job with Boeing. John enjoys this car very much and it is his daily driver for the 35-mile round trip to work in Everett, Wash., each day.

Since it has a 232-cid six-cylinder engine, it is reasonably economical.

John is president of the Puget Sound AMC Club. The members appreciate that he was born and raised in Kenosha, home of AMC and Nash. John enjoys telling fellow AMC club members about his visits to Kenosha and finding Ramblers and driving them back to Washington state. He's done that twice so far -- with a '64 Rambler Typhoon (limited edition) and a '51 Nash Statesman. Both cars made it with no major problems.

John has one Nash and three Ramblers now and enjoys the connection they provide to his hometown of Kenosha.

Keith and Carol Gumbinger's 1949 Ford "woodie" wagon, which showcases Ford's first all-new post-war styling.

John and Pauline Gumbinger's 1966 AMC Rambler Classic 770 station wagon. This car is Washington state resident John's link to his birthplace of Kenosha where AMC products were produced.

Hardtop Hauler

Bob Bakinowski of Tucson, Ariz., is the owner of this 1957 Oldsmobile Fiesta Super 88 station wagon. The Fiesta has over 250,000 miles on its clock and, according to its owner, all that has been done to it since new is a repaint in 1972 and the rear bumper was rechromed in 1989.

Built For Speed and Cargo

by Jack Stutz
Eugene, Oregon

In the spring of 1955, I was about to graduate from high school and my parents and I were considering the joint purchase of a new car.

Since my parents had driven a 1939 Chevrolet from 1942 to 1950, as well as several other Chevys during their lifetime, they were leaning toward a new Chevy. I, on the other hand, had grown up with the idea that V-8 Fords were the way to go and I owned a 1947 Ford V-8 at the time.

After some discussion, my parents and I agreed to buy a new Ford station wagon and trade in my 1947 Ford. We ordered the new wagon during May and took delivery in June 1955. It was a blue and white Country Sedan with a 182-hp Power Pack V-8 with four-barrel carburetor and dual exhaust, Fordomatic transmission, radio, heater, tinted glass and full wheelcovers. The retail price was $3,192.20.

We thought that we would take the car to go hunting and fishing but it didn't take me long to decide that it was too nice for that kind of use. Of course, my parents didn't have the same view on the car's use so we decided to dissolve the joint venture and I started making all of the loan payments. I soon changed the dual exhaust stock mufflers to glass packs.

I enjoyed the summer, fall and winter of 1955 with a new car, but in the spring of 1956 I joined the U.S. Navy. I had little time or money for a new car so my parents drove the car for two years and helped with the loan payments. In 1958, I returned from the Navy and resumed control of the Ford.

During the next few years, I made several modifications to the car, such as installing a McCulloch super-charger. Later, the supercharger was removed and a triple two-barrel manifold and a Spalding flame thrower ignition was installed. I next purchased a 1956 Thunderbird 292-cid V-8 and three-speed transmission. The 292 received a .180 bore job, Clay Smith cam, heavy valve springs and four-barrel manifold. This created a good-running 312-cid Ford V-8 with a short stroke, which, along with the three-speed transmission, was dropped into the wagon.

In September 1959, I became married and drove this car on my honeymoon. In 1965, I sold this car with the built-up Thunderbird engine to a younger brother. After some time, he blew the engine and I helped him reinstall the original 272-cid engine, which I still had.

My brother later acquired a Ford 427-cid / 425-hp engine and C-6 automatic transmission, which he installed in the car. Needless to say, the car performed well with this combination. He later removed the engine and transmission for another project and the Ford sat for about 20 years waiting to be rebuilt.

In 1992, my wife and I bought back the car from my brother and started a complete rebuild.

The wagon has been repainted the original blue and white. It has a new interior featuring a combination of vinyl and cloth in various shades of blue. It also has new chrome, new tinted glass and we have installed a Ford 302-cid V-8, C-4 automatic transmission, power steering, custom wheels and a lowered front end.

The wagon has the original license plates issued by Oregon, when new, and has the original key holder made of leather that was provided by the local Ford dealer when sold new.

The restored and customized 1955 Ford Country Sedan that Jack Stutz, or a member of his family, has owned since purchased-new. The car is displayed with its original issue Oregon plates and dealer-issued leather key fob.

Not a Tire Kicker!

by Harry Bishop
Santee, California

A humorous situation I recall involves my 250-pound friend and his four large teenage boys and large wife purchasing a new 1958 Edsel station wagon.

They all piled in at the curb and started to leave the dealer's place and the wagon would not move. The car body had settled on the tires, which prevented them from going anywhere. They got their money back, but I do not know what car they ended up with.

Coffee Pot Express(o)

Charles Halpin III of Elkins Park, Pa., recalls: "Sunshine, beach and sand were the ingredients for our summer vacations at the Jersey shore in the late 1950s and early 1960s. The entire family, including our dog Niplah, loaded into our 1957 Ford Country Squire station wagon to travel the 90-mile distance to the shore. The photograph shows my mother, Betty Halpin, before one of these excursions, circa 1961. The passenger list included my father, Charlie, and nine children. As my mother remembers: 'During these trips I always held a baby in my lap with the coffee pot at my feet.'"

Lost and Found

by Ray Smith
Tecumseh, Michigan

My arrival in Southeast Michigan during the winter of 1993-'94 from my home state of Massachusetts had been preceded by a protracted and rather messy divorce from my first wife as well as a settlement of a personal injury case that had left me with several extra dollars to spend on a car. It was also the beginning of a new life with my first true love, whom I had met 30 years prior while serving in the armed forces.

After settling into our new (to us) home, I began the long and tedious search for my "new" old car. Having owned several station wagons and sedan deliveries in the past (Chevrolets, Ford Pintos, and even an Austin Cooper Mini), it was within the realm of possibility that I might choose another.

One day as I flipped through a local trader paper, I spotted an ad for a 1955 Pontiac Star Chief Custom Safari Wagon, fully restored, with what seemed like a reasonable asking price.

I phoned the owner and he seemed surprised that I was calling about the car. It seems that he had placed the ad well over a year previous and had received no response whatsoever. He had been thinking of placing a new ad in another paper the same day I had called.

He described the vehicle in honest terms, detailing its faults as well as its good points. It sounded pretty good so I made an appointment for my wife and I to make the three-hour drive to see the car.

It was a cold day and the owner's house was out in the middle of farm country. As we drove across the little bridge to his house and barn, I spied the Safari sitting out front idling. He had pulled it out of the barn and had gotten it ready for a test drive.

After showing me all of the details he had described over the phone, I took it for a short hop around the block (several miles in this case). It really wasn't necessary. I knew from the moment I laid eyes on it I would own it. I've had that same feeling for every car I have ever owned.

A price was reached that was agreeable to both of us and two weeks later, he delivered it to my front door. Since that day, my wife and I have racked up well over 30,000 miles of pleasurable motoring with few mechanical problems. The car is a joy to drive (especially with the new radial tires we installed), and we are looking forward to our fourth excursion to New England in the near future.

Ray Smith's 1955 Pontiac Star Chief Custom Safari, which he has customized by adding pin striping and graphics.

Ray Smith's 1957 Pontiac Star Chief Custom Safari, on which he painted graphics in 1963 only to accidentally happen upon the car for sale some 30 years later and buy it.

According to Ray Smith, this is "The pair that will be beat a full house any day of the week." His Pontiac Safari wagons, a 1957 (left) and 1955, respectively.

Which brings us to the "Great Smith Station Wagon Saga, Part II."

It was on one of our annual treks to New England that I became the owner of Safari number two. A little background:

Having been a pin striper since the age of 14, I had built a good business in the Boston area over the years, also acquiring in the process many friends and acquaintances who are also certifiable car nuts.

One of these friends had been constructing a 1932 Ford phaeton for a number of years and it finally looked as if it were to be finished. In speaking of my impending trip, he asked if I could bring my painting kit, as he really wanted me to stripe the Ford.

When I finally showed up at his shop driving the Safari (he had never seen it before), he mentioned that he had a friend who owned a car similar and that it was for sale. Needless to say, my curiosity was piqued. Knowing that Safaris were not made in great quantities (fewer than 10,000 for the three years they were produced), I wanted to see this car.

We contacted the owner (who worked for the Post Office and was on his day off), and went over to see the car. He lived on one of the many hidden side streets of a Boston suburb and the car was stored across the street in one of a row of low cinder block garages.

It took an hour for him to find the garage key and another with a can of spray lube to open the somewhat stubborn lock. We finally got it open and swung back the doors to reveal the blue nose of a 1957 Pontiac. At this point, I wasn't sure it was a Safari because most of the car was buried beneath a pile of old cardboard boxes, green trash bags, and several old bicycle frames.

At this point, I need to digress with some background information. During the early 1960s, a friend of mine had put together a '57 Safari drag car. It was painted the original Cordova brown (red) and white, had all new suspension and brake pieces, a 421-cid Pontiac engine with dual four-barrel carburetors, headers, roller cam and dual coil ignition.

Just before I went into the service (1963) I had done some paint work on this car. Jerry (the owner) wanted something simple: the word "Safari" in script above the glovebox, which I was happy to do. He had campaigned the car for a couple of years and finally sold it and moved on to other things. I saw the car once afterward and it had sported a new blue paint job.

As I stood there looking at the front of this car, I wondered to myself, "Could this be Jerry's old car?" A funny feeling started up inside me.

We managed to clear away the trash enough for me to get to the driver's side door. The garage was narrow and I hoped I could open the door wide enough to get inside to look at the floors. By opening the door and rolling down the window, I managed to crawl inside. The first thing that greeted me was the woodgrained formica piece used to cover the original instrument placements. In the two pods were a Stewart-Warner tach and speedometer. Looking further across I spied a Hurst shifter and a cluster of four gauges hanging loosely under the dashboard. Further still my eyes came to rest on that fa-

miliar (and a trifle amateurish) script painted above the glovebox that simply read "Safari" exactly as I had painted it on that long gone day in the summer of 1963! The memory came rushing back! Now it really didn't matter what the rest of the car was like; I wanted it!

We went to a nearby coffee shop and talked for a while about cars and our experiences over the years, and eventually came to a figure agreeable to both of us. I had to leave the car there for the winter, but drove out in the spring to pick it up. Before coming, I phoned my friend Don (who had originally told me about the car), and he got it out of the garage and on four inflated tires. Amazingly, after 17 years of sitting in the garage, not only did the original tires (installed in 1966) hold air, but the brakes still functioned. Even more amazing, the Delco air shocks still functioned! The owner's method of long-term storage was simple: Back it into the garage, take out the key, and lock the garage door!

The car was amazingly intact. The only rust was in one rocker panel (a six-inch long piece). The original 13.5:1 compression race engine had lost a piston and had been replaced with a stock (salvage yard) 389-cid V-8 with four-barrel carb. The owner still had the dual four-barrel manifold, but unfortunately the rare W&H Du-coil ignition was gone. (I did get a cap and rotor for it in one of the boxes of parts.) The M-22 close-ratio four-speed transmission, aluminum flywheel and clutch, Ansen two-piece scatter shield and 4.56 Posi rear were still installed in the car as well as the beautifully constructed exhaust headers and collectors that fit so tightly up underneath the car they cannot be seen from the side.

The trip my son and I took to retrieve the car is quite another story. Needless to say, it involved driving nonstop at a rather high rate of speed in a four-wheel-drive truck that consumed fuel similar to a Sherman tank.

In the time since I brought this Pontiac back to Michigan, I have managed to get it running (the engine sounds like a 55-gallon drum full of psychotic woodpeckers) and the oil pressure varies more than the weather here). Driving through town (sneaking, actually) with loud exhaust and the almost non-existent suspension jarring loose every filling in my teeth, with people staring at this unkempt looking vehicle with its scratched paint and rusty wheels (and sprayed-on vinyl roof), with its equally unkempt driver with long, scraggily hair (and a huge grin on his bearded face) and holding their kids a little closer to them, and the driver feeling as if he was 16 years old again driving his old (and unregistered) car and hoping the cops are not around. Hey, it doesn't get much better than that!

Anyway, the '57 Safari is now under roof with its brother Safari and is slowly being made roadworthy again. The 4.56 gears have been replaced by a more reasonable 3.08 gearset and the tired engine by a 1965 389-cid V-8 with TH400 transmission that has but 12,000 original miles. It will hopefully be complete enough to drive soon and possibly take back to New England. Maybe I can then go about the re-restoration of the '55 Safari, which is starting to show its age once more. Or maybe I could do the '55 Pontiac hearse my friend brought back from Colorado and says I can't do without. Or maybe ....

Park It Behind the Porsche

by D. Leroy Decker
Riverton, Utah

My wife and I recently completed the restoration of a white 1965 Dodge Coronet 440 four-door station wagon.

The Dodge's initial need of replacement freeze plugs and lower front end parts turned into a water pump, differential driveline seal, brake lines, valve adjustment, tune up, and new white paint to match the original. Also, we re-chromed the roof rails and other trim, and installed new taillamp lenses. We converted the front bench seat to bucket seats, redesigned the upholstery, added a console, changed the wheelcovers and installed the only lazy Susan-style storage where the rear seat lies hidden beneath.

While I was registering, Mopar lovers were inviting my wife to park the wagon in their section at a recent show at the University of Utah. We entered our wagon and Thunderbird and had lots of people talk to us about their interest in station wagons. We are not trophy seekers; we just enjoy car shows, cruises and restoring vehicles. My wife used to own a Mercury station wagon and I previously owned Chevy wagons of the '50s and '60s. We are members of the Thunderbird Motor Club of Utah with our 1963 convertible and fond of our '63 Falcon convertible.

The Dodge wagon was so unsightly when I acquired it that my wife asked me not to put it in our Ford garage! But she's had her Porsche in there and I've always been fond of the Mopars. I have owned a Dodge Monaco and dreamed of acquiring a Roadrunner and Charger. So I settled for a wagon!

Leroy Decker's 1965 Dodge Coronet 440 station wagon, which he and his wife recently restored.

Part of the restoration of the Decker's Dodge wagon included the installation of a "lazy Susan-style storage where the rear seat lies hidden beneath."

Thank the Chauffeur

by Harvey McEwen
White Rock, British Columbia, Canada

I had often viewed the 1953 Buick Roadmaster Estate Wagon parked beside the famous 1939 McLaughlin Buick 'Royal Tour' Convertible Sedan (1939 King and Queen visit to Canada) in the carriage house of a beautiful estate located near Victoria on Vancouver Island. During the early 1960s, my interest was only in the convertible, but of course, as time went by, the "woodie" wagon, because of its rarity and superb original virgin condition, became of intense interest to me.

Years rolled by and in 1987, the Buick was ours. It had 74,000 miles, three burned valves, a leaky brake system, and no action for 14 years.

We did what was needed, plus polished the original Mandarin red paint and chrome. The interior is perfect original, even the factory rubber floor mat. All wood is very good. It was optioned with factory wire wheel covers, spotlight with mirror and dealer roof rack. The wagon was used as a summer vacation vehicle, hence, its good condition (chauffeur maintained). The body was built by Ionia, and this is the last year of real wood bodies and the first year of the new V-8 engine.

There were 670 Roadmaster station wagons built. The estimated number of survivors--maybe two dozen.

During the 1950s, you could spot a Buick from a far distance due to its toothy grille.

The original chauffeur of the 1953 Buick Roadmaster Estate Wagon, Bob Cameron, seeing the car for the final time. Betty McEwen, wife of the car's new owner, Harvey McEwen, is shown driving the Buick onto the transporter.

Harvey and Betty McEwen's 1953 Buick Roadmaster Estate Wagon as it looks today, with original Mandarin red finish and wood as well as original interior. The car was chauffeur maintained and reflects the fine care it received from Bob Cameron through the years.

The all-original interior of the Roadmaster appears as if the car recently rolled off the assembly line.

After the Buick was in storage for 14 years, there was lots of dust. Both the wood and original paint finish were in fine shape under that layer of dust.

The engine was pulled out and overhauled. The firewall and engine compartment were cleaned up with no repainting necessary.

Bring On the Mountains

by John Schmitt
Milwaukee, Wisconsin

I purchased my '55 Ford Country Squire station wagon, serial #U5PY190689, new from Al Shallock Ford in Milwaukee, Wis., on Oct. 23, 1955. The total price was $3,279.50. The car's color is Mountain green.

It has a 272-cid V-8 engine with four-barrel carburetor, and has 7.6:1 compression and dual exhaust. It has a Fordomatic transmission, power steering, radio, heater, clock, map light, tissue dispenser, fog lights, full wheelcovers, carpeting, top carrier and whitewall tires.

The interior is all original. The paint is 90 percent original, with touch-up only around the wheel wells and rocker panels, and no rust.

This car has been driven 88,467 miles. The engine has never been overhauled, and the transmission was rebuilt in 1996. It has been a good car. It was used primarily as a family car, pulling a Nimrod camping trailer most of the time. We had a lot of fun with this car on many vacation trips, traveling to most of the mountains in the United States with up to seven kids aboard. It went on many hunting trips to the Dakotas for pheasants and Wisconsin for deer until 1974, when I bought a pickup truck.

In 1975, I purchased collector plates. Since then, the Ford is used mainly for car shows and is driven to all the shows. It has been awarded 15 trophies in the last two years. It is still fun to drive!

John Schmitt's 1955 Ford Country Squire station wagon, which he purchased new from Shallock Ford in Milwaukee, Wis.

Wagonaire Waterfall

by Tom Acker
Twentynine Palms, California

Being Studebaker lovers, my wife Millie and I have owned a Studebaker of one model or other since 1940.

In 1966, we saw a 1963 Studebaker Lark Wagonaire for sale. We bought it for $400 and drove it home. It had been repainted an olive drab military color.

After several weeks of work cleaning off the old paint, we painted it white and golden brown with double white striping. We drove this wagon until 1997 when, one day, it blew its engine. We sold it as is for $500 to a fellow who said he wanted to restore it.

Two special features of the Wagonaire I wish to emphasize are that it was always an interesting style leader and is often unrecognized by many young persons. Secondly, it had a slide-away rear roof panel that allowed you to open the cargo area like a pick-up truck, which was handy for odd-shaped hauling. The most interesting thing of this feature was the sliding track the top moved forward on. Once the weather seals became old, they would allow rain water to seep into this track, which ended above the two front seats. The result was quite invigorating! Whenever you stopped the car, all the water that had seeped into the tracks would rush forward and go directly down the back of your neck. I never had a single case of ring around the collar thanks to our nice little Wagonaire.

Oh yes, as small as it seemed, I also installed the six-way power seat of a 1963 Lincoln Continental in place of the old Studebaker bench seat proving that the inside of that little Wagonaire was as large as a Lincoln.

Tom and Millie Acker's modified 1963 Studebaker Lark Wagonaire station wagon. The Ackers purchased the Wagonaire for $400 in 1966 and sold it for $500 in 1997 with its engine blown after 30+ years of faithful hauling service.

Nation Cruiser

by John Shipley
Tigard, Oregon

I own a 1971 Mercury Montego MX Villager station wagon. I purchased the car in 1980 for $200. I have driven the car 200,000 miles without incident, including five trips West Coast to East Coast round trip. The wagon is powered by a 351-cid V-8, with four-barrel carburetor, coupled to a C-6 automatic transmission. It has a limited slip rear as well as power windows.

I am slowly restoring the car. Only 2,121 MX Villagers were produced in 1971. I have taken the Mercury to more than a few car shows, and have received many offers from people wanting to buy the wagon!

John Shipley's $200, 200,000-mile 1971 Mercury Montego MX Villager station wagon. He has driven the car on five coast to coast trips since 1980.

From Travel Agent to Tractor

by Gary Vanier
Auburn, California

I have owned a 1967 Ford Country Squire nine-passenger station wagon with 390-cid engine for 30 years. The car began life as a modern day "depot hack" on the peninsula in the bay area of northern California. It was ordered with what Ford called the "taxi" package, which included oversize brakes and cooling system and heavy-duty suspension. Being a nine-passenger wagon this car has the "Magic Doorgate" and the extra side mount seats and lockable storage compartment.

The Ford was built in late 1966. It was leased to a Burlingame travel agency in 1967 to drive passengers from the agency to the San Francisco Airport. It was kept at the travel agency and, I was told, never taken home or used for other purposes by the owners of the agency. It was turned in at the end of the year, which was when I purchased it from the lease company, Engs Motor Trucks of San Francisco.

As a result of not being used too often this car had low mileage when I purchased it and was more new than used.

Over the years this car has been all over the United States and Canada and has pulled a 30-foot Airstream trailer and 18-foot speedboat. The wagon is mostly original although the engine has been rebuilt.

In the 1970s, this wagon covered over 10,000 miles on one trip during a six week period, traveling through the northwestern United States and Western Canada pulling the Airstream trailer the entire distance with no trouble.

Over the years, while loyally serving our family this faithful wagon succeeded where others failed.

When both this wagon and I were younger I was visiting my parents one cold winter day and my dad insisted I plow two acres of field at his place before I left. I went out to start the tractor, but due to the cold and damp, try as I might, I could not start the tractor.

I decided to hook the plow to the hitch on the Ford, put the C-6 transmission in low gear and plow the field.

The wagon pulled the plow as well as the tractor and with much more comfort with radio music blaring!

Another time, our family met at the family cabin in the California Sierras. It snowed heavy during dinner, and after dinner my brother-in-law decided to go to town. He was not gone long from the cabin before he returned and said his new four-wheel-drive Chevy Blazer was stuck. Once a cable was hooked to the wagon and the C-6 transmission put in low gear, the Blazer was pulled from its resting place in short order (a feat my teenage nieces never let my brother-in-law forget).

This old wagon is still used and enjoyed by our family in the "Gold Country" of northern California.

Gary Vanier's 1967 Ford Country Squire station wagon has pulled big and small camping trailers, a speedboat and, incredibly, a stalled tractor to help plow a field. The car is powered by a 390-cid V-8.

"Thunder Wagon"

by Ted Pisarek, Jr.
Syracuse, New York

"Thunder Wagon" is our 1969 Pontiac Bonneville nine-passenger station wagon with 428-cid/360-hp V-8, 400 automatic, positraction, and heavy-duty suspension. I purchased the car at an auto auction (I'm a used car dealer) on a cold February night in 1983. My intention, as with all the cars I buy, was to repair, clean, polish and sell it. Somewhere along the line, I lost control. The more I worked on this car the more I realized that if anyone deserved to own this great car it was me.

In the time we have owned this wagon, I have either replaced, repaired, restored, remanufactured, repacked, readjusted, reworked, repainted, disassembled, reassembled, cleaned and polished everything. There is a special room in our cellar just for the Pontiac's "stuff" (extra parts, cleaners, polishes, etc.), and a file cabinet for literature and related articles.

My wife, B.J., and I have given up our Saturdays to scrounge through salvage yards for used parts, including one time in the rain, mud, and cow manure. I belong to car clubs, subscribe to collector car magazines, and spend my weekends at car shows. Our vacations are spent at car shows instead of 100 Islands, Florida or Mexico.

All winter I am forced to brush snow and ice off my daily driver because "Thunder Wagon" is in the garage (winter storage you know). As I said, I've lost control!

The Bonneville wagon was originally from Manheim, Pa., but I was told the car also spent time in Florida at the original owner's second home. I am fortunate that the previous owner liked accessories; it has eight standard Bonneville features and 31 optional accessories. Base price on the Bonneville nine-passenger wagon was $4,199.50 and after adding the 31 options the price increased to $6,215.29 -- and that was almost 30 years ago!

Pontiac definitely built a great road car, six adults and all their luggage, just put some air in the shocks and with 428 cubic inches you do not even notice the load. Of course, the 360 horsepower tend to consume gas, 9 mpg city/14 mpg highway (with the air on), but it's a small price to pay.

There were 7,428 Bonneville station wagons produced in 1969, and using the standard rule of thumb that 10 percent of a model and year survive, I might have a rare car not to mention all the options making it a rarer model still. I have only seen one other and it was in a salvage yard near Rochester, New York.

Ted Pisarek, Jr.'s 1969 Pontiac Bonneville station wagon, equipped with a 428-cid/360-hp V-8. Because of the big-block power, the wagon has been aptly nicknamed the "Thunder Wagon."

Another Chance

by Robert Headrick, Jr.
St. Louis, Missouri

I bought my first 1954 Chevrolet (a Bel Air convertible) in the spring of 1989. This was the beginning of my love for the '54 Chevrolets. Right after buying the convertible, I began to collect other models of the '54 Chevrolet. But, the most difficult one to find was the Bel Air Townsman eight-passenger station wagon.

I watched for and responded to several ads over the next five years, but each time the wagon advertised turned out to be a 210 or 150 model. A couple of times the sellers had added the unmistakable Bel Air trim (painted side spears with the Bel Air tag), but in the process of attempting to create a Bel Air Townsman wagon they failed to realize that there were several characteristics that were unique to the Townsman wagons: sliding rear windows, Bel Air body trim, three seats and the unique imitation woodgrain trim. Thus, each time I found what appeared from an ad to be a Townsman wagon was, in actuality, not the "real McCoy."

In July 1994, I was reading *Old Cars Weekly* when I spotted an ad that offered for sale a 1954 Bel Air station wagon. Like before, I got especially nervous just prior to making the call. This time I was especially nervous be-

Robert Headrick, Jr.'s 1954 Chevrolet Bel Air Townsman station wagon prior to undergoing restoration. After searching for several years to find a Townsman, he now has two of the Bel Air wagons.

cause the ad stipulated a "Bel Air" wagon -- most ads before just read, "1954 Chevrolet station wagon." I called the number in the ad, and I asked just two questions: "Did this car have three seats?" and "Was there imitation woodgrain?" The answer to each question was "Yes." Eureka! I had found the real thing!

I could hardly control myself. I told the owner that I would like to come and look at the car prior to deciding if I wanted to buy it. That was fine. I made plans to go the following weekend, but, just before setting out to see the car, I called to get the directions and the owner told me he had sold the car just a day before. I was disappointed.

I continued to look for a Townsman wagon. A year later, in July 1995, I was again reading the classifieds in *Old Cars Weekly* when I again ran across an ad offering a 1954 Bel Air station wagon; could it be? I called and asked the same two questions. This time, I spoke with the owner's wife and she took the time to run and look in the garage in order to confirm that the car had three seats, it bore Bel Air on the sides, and that it did, indeed, have imitation woodgrain. This time, I said I would take it ... without even looking at it. The owner's wife insisted that I see it before agreeing to buy it. I agreed to look at photos they would send me, but I also said I would send a down payment so that they would hold the car until I had a chance to see the photos.

A week or so later, the photos arrived. It was indeed a 1954 Bel Air Townsman. What was even more ironic was that it was the same car I had missed a chance to buy the summer before.

Two weeks later a transport company picked up the car and delivered it to me in Missouri. It drove like a gem, but it needed some work: paint, minor body work, some rechroming, the imitation wood redone and detailing and cleaning of the interior. I drove the car the rest of the summer; it was a blast! By early fall, I'd decided to have it restored. I sought out a restorer with experience in cars with woodgraining. I found one and took the car to him in November (a 12 hour trip--the car ran like a charm the entire way!).

This is where the story becomes unbelievable. After checking references and getting all the information I thought I needed in order to judge the qualifications of the shop I took the car to for restoration purposes, I discovered that the owner of the shop was not legitimate (but, that's another story). Suffice it to say, three years later, I managed to get my car out of the shop and, unfortunately, the work done was poor and required someone to do it all over. Yes, a few thousand dollars later, the car was off again to yet another restoration shop. Now, almost five years after a minor restoration was begun, a full restoration of my 1954 Townsman nears completion.

The car is Bermuda green with two-tone dark/light green interior. There were originally 8,156 Townsman wagons produced, approximately 1.68 percent of the Bel Airs produced (486,240) in 1954.

In July 1996, I bought another Townsman and this one is undergoing a total restoration. This wagon, purchased in Georgia, has power steering, power brakes, power seat and power windows, as well as several other dealer-installed options. It will probably be one-of-a-kind when completed. It is Horizon blue and India Ivory.

Siren is $85 Option

by Lloyd Ray
Council Bluffs, Iowa

Our 1962 Chevrolet Bel Air station wagon conversion ambulance is rare. It was built by Cotner/Bevington Corp. of Blytheville, Ark. It has a raised roof and one-piece rear door. Included is the factory list of options from Cotner/Bevington. As shown, the conversion modifications made the delivered price of the Chevy pretty steep. Cotner/Bevington only made these coaches for about three years on Chevy chassis. After 1964, conversions were mainly based on Buick, Oldsmobile or Pontiac chassis.

My wife, Karen, and I currently own five Chevrolet station wagons: a 1954 Bel Air Townsman eight-passenger wagon, two 1958s – a Nomad and Yeoman – the 1962 ambulance and a 1970 Caprice Kingswood Estate wagon.

The data plate shows the Bel Air-to-ambulance conversion took place on May 3, 1962.

Lloyd and Karen Ray's 1962 Chevrolet Bel Air station wagon ambulance conversion. The "amblewagon" features a one-piece rear door instead of a factory tailgate as well as a raised roof. The conversion was performed by Cotner/Bevington Corp. of Arkansas, which explains the unique "CB" script behind the front wheelwell. The Bel Air is powered by a 327-cid/ 300-hp V-8.

Station Wagon Conversions
• NOT EXTENDED •

More Inside Height

More Inside Length

Date_____

Price List for conversions and accessories for Station Wagon to Professional Cars and Ambulances.

Chassis Model_____

NAME PLATES: To Read_____

NOTE: If it's for an Ambulance, Funeral Coach or Family Car we can furnish it. Write Today for Information.

	EXTRA ACCESSORIES	$	$			EXTRA ACCESSORIES	$	$
1	Install new roof for additional headroom	795.00	✔		42	Federal beacon ray light No. 17	85.00	✔
2	Rear door hinged on side as regular ambulance door, approx. 6" extra length is gained	680.00	✔		43	Federal beacon ray light No. 17-D	95.00	
3	Ambulance type floor installed in rear compartment covered with Armstrong inlaid linoleum over ¾" plywood over steel floor with fold down attendant's seat installed in ambulance type rear floor with compartment under floor	282.50			44	Jr. Federal beacon ray light	65.00	
					45	Magnetic beacon ray light, plugs in cigarette lighter	62.50	
4	Thin Partition between front and rear compartments with sliding glass window	185.00			46	Federal No. 28 siren, mounted under hood	75.00	✔
5	Split 2nd seat, ⅓ may be used by attendant	195.00	✔		47	Federal EG siren, mounted under hood	55.00	
6	Paint complete car customer's choice of color where rear door and new roof are installed.	97.50			48	Federal Model C-6 with propello-ray light with brake	210.00	
7	Paint complete car customer's choice of color where rear door and roof are not installed	150.00			49	Federal Model WL siren combination with red flashing light, mounted on roof or fender	77.50	
8	Two bucket type front seats right seat swivel type, exchange price for standard front seat	275.00			50	Rear compartment heater	85.00	
9	Removable plexiglass ambulance signs for rear quarter windows	65.00	✔		51	Rear corner marking lights, pair	29.50	
10	Roller shades, per window, Installed	13.50			52	Flasher motor for red lights	24.50	
11	Airplane style drapes, per window, Installed (5)	19.50	97.50		53	Thompson portable spot light, with 100 feet of cord	65.00	
12	Combination storage compartment and oxygen tank holder between the two bucket seats	57.50			54	Roto-Beam light, stationary type	65.00	
13	Removable first aid compartment	47.50	✔		55	Rear loading light, hooked up to come on with rear door	27.50	✔
14	Overhead first aid and storage compartment	67.50			56	Hook up Back-up lights to come on when rear door is open	19.50	✔
15	Removable twin type casket table, with pins	97.50			57	Spot light clear lens	29.95	
16	Floor skid bars, full set	65.00			58	Extra dome light, each	17.50	✔
17	Carpet for rear, stationary or removable snap-on	97.50			59	Special low Washington cot, Model 409	119.00	
18	48-inch rubber mat for rear compartment	47.50	✔		60	Special low Washington two-level cot, Model 54-L	143.50	
19	Inlaid linoleum over rear floor	65.00			61	Sponge rubber mattress, with waterproof cover	39.75	
20	Nameplate sockets, per pair of nameplates	12.50			62	Ferno one-man cot, with 3" mattress	298.00	
21	Nameplates, pr., 16 letters with mounting sockets Each additional letter over 16	24.95 1.00	✔		63	Ferno all-level cot, with mattress	185.00	
22	Nameplates for outside mounting	29.50			64	Washington folding stretcher, on wheels and legs	46.00	
23	Removable oxygen tank holder	16.50			65	Cot Hook, removable type Side mounting type	47.50	✔
24	Fan for rear compartment	24.50						
25	Quart fire extinguisher	24.00			66	Installation of customers cot hook	27.50	
26	Roof ventilator	24.50			67	Delco-Remy 105 amp. alternator	275.00	
27	Rear door window chrome	45.00			68	Washington Stair Chair No. 40	47.50	
28	Zipper in headliner where roof is raised	7.50	✔		69	Converting Station Wagon to Landau Style No. C-60H-35	270.00	
29	Emerson utility resuscitator, less cylinders	290.00			70	Converting to Style No. P-61-26	200.00	
30	Emerson dual utility resuscitator, less cylinders	410.00			71	Landau Bow, Chrome	75.00	
31	Oxygen "D" cylinders, each	23.50			72	Landau Bow, Painted	60.00	
32	Installing customer's siren, red lights, beacon ray, etc.	29.50			73	Puerto Rico Style Emblem	95.00	
33	Provisions in roof headliner for removable siren or red light, where roof is not raised.	27.50			74	Landau Interior Trim	69.50	
34	Pair chrome type tunnel lights on front of roof	95.00			75	Landau Indirect Lights	75.00	
35	Pair chrome type tunnel lights on rear of roof	95.00			76	Full Length Wheel Housings, trimmed to match interior	69.00	
36					77			
37					78			
38					79			
39					80			
40					81			
41					82			
					83			
					TOTAL PRICE		2,231	95
					EXCISE TAX			

Federal excise Mfgrs. tax to be added where applicable.

All delivery agreements are made subject to fire, strikes, government apportionment of raw materials, acts of God and other conditions beyond the control of vendor.

COTNER/BEVINGTON CORPORATION • BLYTHEVILLE, ARKANSAS

The Cotner/Bevington Corp. price list for conversion accessories shows what equipment was added to the Bel Air to increase its factory price by an additional $2,231.95. The $7.50 for the headliner zipper seems a bargain!

Among the five Chevrolet station wagons that Lloyd and Karen Ray own are this 1954 Bel Air Townsman eight-passenger model (above) and a 1958 Nomad four-door wagon, equipped with modern Rallye wheels.

"Orphan Annie"

by Dorsey Lewis
Milwaukie, Oregon

I have owned 50 or so collector cars in my life. In 1955, when I was 14 years old, a great car showed up at Lakeview Sales & Service (Lakeview, Ore.). It was a new DeSoto Firedome station wagon made that year. Sold to Mr. Drinkwater, who was the Flying "A" distributor in Lakeview, for $3,987.65, he and his family drove it until 1968. It was then parked in a cow pasture for 25 years.

Every year when I would go back to my hometown of Lakeview from Portland, Ore., I would stop and attempt to buy the car. For many years I had no luck. Then in 1992, Mr. Drinkwater's son Richard was tired of me working on him and he caved in and sold me the DeSoto.

After sitting for 25 years it was looking a little weathered, but I could still remember what it looked like new. So after three years and a lot of blood, sweat and $$$, I have one of the greatest station wagons ever made, the 1955 DeSoto Firedome that we have nicknamed "Orphan Annie."

This DeSoto wagon was designed by Virgil Exner, and only 1,803 were produced. Its base price was $3,170, making it the most expensive car in the 1955 DeSoto lineup. The Firedome's engine is the 291-cid / 185-hp V-8.

This bill of sale shows the simplicity of the times: a one-page contract that reflects the $3,987.65 price of the 1955 DeSoto Firedome minus the $1,165 price of the trade-in 1950 Dodge four-door sedan. Actual cost to the DeSoto's first owner, Charles Drinkwater, was $2,922.65.

173

Dorsey Lewis is the second owner of this 1955 DeSoto Firedome station wagon. The car is nicknamed "Orphan Annie" and has undergone a complete restoration inside and out.

Found and Lost

by Bob Guckenberger
St. Petersburg, Florida

In 1968, I could no longer resist the temptation to own and restore an old car--particularly a woodie. One Saturday, a local newspaper hit my driveway, and as usual I combed the automobile classifieds. There it was, a '47 Chevrolet station wagon, right in my neighborhood. I immediately drove to the address, only to find another buyer writing a check for $700.

I figured that was that, but in relating my tale of missed opportunity to a collector friend, he gave me a tip on a man in Hyannis, Mass., who had a '48 Buick "woodie" he wanted to sell. I must have made a dozen calls, but each time his wife answered and said he wasn't there. Finally, I asked if there was anywhere I could reach him. "Sure," his wife replied. "He's at Clancy's Bar." I called Clancy's and got the owner of the Buick to the phone. He not only agreed to sell it to me for $300, but would drive it from Hyannis to Syosset, Long Island for only an additional $50. What a deal! I bought it sight unseen.

My wife called me at the office when the wagon arrived at our home. "Are you sure you want me to give him the check?", she asked, adding that the woodie was in sad shape. "A deal is a deal," I replied. "Give him the money." I arrived home expecting the worst. It was worse than the worst!

Somehow the former owner drove it from Massachusetts to Long Island with no wipers (it was snowing that day), a massive shimmy at 50 mph, a broken manifold, balding tires and barely discernible brakes. From being outside, the wood had turned the color of a New England barn and the doors had swollen closed when the car defrosted in my heated garage. To get in, I had to crawl through the window.

"It's not so bad," I declared, knowing better, but not admitting it. And so the restoration began. To get the gray out of the wood, I had to apply several coats of wood bleach. Wood bleach is an acid based concoction

The $350 1948 Buick Roadmaster "woodie" wagon as it was delivered in 1968 after a sight unseen-purchase to the home of Bob Guckenberger. It was complete, but a complete mess!

that seeks out pinhole leaks in industrial strength rubber gloves and sends you screaming to the sink to flush it off. When applied to wood, you can actually see and hear it festering.

After months of bleaching, sanding, staining and varnishing, the Buick was ready for painting. A woodie looks best painted maroon, so I chose that color instead of the original blue. I really didn't know what I had yet, so I opted for what pleased me. Mechanically everything was fixed and the Buick ran beautifully. Batteries, especially six-volters, are a tenuous thing on an old car started just once a week. I used to keep the Buick's big straight-eight running when I got gas to keep it charging, thus avoiding another start. (If you pump quickly, you can keep ahead of the fuel consumption at idle!) One day, a service station attendant (remember them?) asked how the engine ran. I replied, "It's running." I had to open the hood to prove it to him--that's how quiet a Buick straight-eight is.

The Roadmaster was equipped with Dynaflow transmission (or "Dynaslush" as we referred to it). Because of this, even with the mammoth, overhead valve eight, the Buick did not accelerate. Rather, it gathered momentum--slowly.

Although Buick continued building "woodie" station wagons through 1953, the '48 is perhaps the automaker's high water mark. This is simply because it had metal fenders applied to wooden doors. Later models had wood applied to metal doors. The top was also the last

to be constructed from wooden slats running from the windshield header to the tailgate and covered with a simulated leather material. Looking up at the top, it appeared to be the bottom of a canoe--a gorgeous array of highly varnished oak.

Our woodie drew many admiring glances and smiles when the "Dewey's Great in '48" bumper sticker was noticed. But it really wasn't collectible, yet. I brought it to a Greater New York Region AACA Meet and an official sniffed, "Put it in the public parking lot, it's not eligible for this show."

So when I found a cherry 1933 Chevrolet Master Eagle rumbleseat three-window coupe with mint original interior, I bought it and put the Buick up for sale. After all, the Chevy could be exhibited at shows and did not require yearly varnishing. Instead of the wagon itself, I brought a picture of it to Hershey and put it on my friend's swap space table. It sold for the asking price of $1,895, which is not a bad investment when the labor involved is discounted.

Later, I discovered that only 320 Roadmaster "woodies" were built in 1948! This was probably the rarest car at that AACA meet where we were denied entrance. Then I saw a full-page ad in *Hemmings Motor News* for a '48 Roadmaster "woodie" with a price of $20,000! Over the ad was stamped "Sorry, sold before publication." It was only a few years after I had parted with mine. Could this be my wagon? I guess I will never know (or want to know). I do know I miss it more than any collector car I have owned and sold since.

After much work cleaning up the Buick cosmetically, as well as some mechanical repairs, Bob Guckenberger's 1948 "woodie" was transformed into a show car—although it was denied access to the showgrounds of a major 1968 meet in New York due to it being not collectible! The bumper sticker in the window reads: "Dewey's Great in '48" to commemorate that year's famous Presidential race.

The Edsel Made Me Do It

by Russ Waterhouse
Newcastle, Washington

It was Saturday morning, 4:30 a.m., May 1959, Memorial Day weekend. I was 14 years old and anticipating a weekend at the beach clam digging. Neither I, nor my parents were prepared for the events that followed in the next six hours that would forever change our lives, especially mine. The next six hours would alter, in fact, dictate my life in my later years. I became an Edsel station wagon nut.

My father, mother, seven-year-old brother and I piled into our 1957 Ford Country Sedan wagon. Our destination was to one of Washington state's fabulous beaches to dig the elusive razor clam. To dig a razor clam you have to be on the beach about thirty minutes before low tide. You look for a dimple in the sand, and dig with an elongated shovel aptly named a "clam gun." It seemed like the worse the weather, the better the digging. The razor clam can travel at three feet per minute almost straight down in the tidal sand. Speed with the "clam gun" is essential. If you do not get it in the first ten seconds, you won't, as the hole keeps caving in. You get wet, cold and sand in places that you cannot imagine. Still, it's fun and such good eating. Driving time from our home near Seattle should have been about four hours to the beach.

Twenty miles from the town of Aberdeen, Wash., on what was then a two lane road it happened. My dad got impatient with traffic. He slammed the shifter into second gear, and floored the gas pedal, waking up that big (?) Thunderbird V-8. He darted left to pass a string of "slow pokes." I will never forget the next seven seconds. BANG, WHUMP, SPEEEE, HISssss. I looked out the rear window and saw nothing. No cars, no fields, no fences, no road, just smoke. White smoke, nothing but a huge cloud of white smoke. Dad coasted to the side of the road--the Ford was dead. A true case of Found On Road Dead.

How the tow truck got there so fast is still a mystery to me. Maybe it was the smoke signal. I remember riding in the car while hooked to the tow truck (try that today!) and enjoying it. My brother and I were probably the only ones having fun at this time.

The tow driver took us to a Lincoln-Mercury-Edsel dealership in Aberdeen to have the car fixed. It was now about 8 a.m. The tow driver alerted the owner of the dealership that we were coming. He was there to meet us as the tow truck dropped us off.

We were asked to wait in an office next to the showroom floor while dad and mom waited to get a total of the damage to the Ford. The dealer priced the parts for the cost for the repairs. My brother and I were looking at the new Mercurys and Edsels that were in the showroom.

Damage to the '57 Ford was extensive. Two of the blades of the fan had broken off. One broken blade had hit the hood with such force that it looked as if an ax had struck it from the underside with no repent. The other blade continued to the right to sever the car's battery in

half. The centrifugal force of the out-of-balance water pump tore it from the engine and smashed its way almost through the radiator. The cost of a new radiator alone was over $200.

Things were bleak to say the least. Saturday morning of a three day weekend, no transportation, no place open to get parts until Tuesday, and over 100 miles from home. Tuesday we had to be back in school, mom and dad had to be back to work. Also, a huge repair bill was going to need to be paid on the car, not to mention bus fare to Seattle and time off work to get the car back home again.

Unable to come up with a solution for the seemingly insurmountable problem at hand my mother looked across the showroom and said, "Oh heck, why don't we just drive one of these home instead."

That was all the dealer needed to hear. Which one, was the big decision. I wanted the big green Mercury that had a $4,000-plus price tag, or the Edsel two-door hardtop priced at a little over $3,500. Dad opted for the Edsel Villager six-passenger wagon that sat beside the hardtop on the showroom floor. This Edsel had only one option, the heater/defroster, and was priced at about $3,000 (1959 was the first year manufacturers were required by law to post their prices on the windows). I found out in my later years that dad traded the Ford "as is" and $800 for the new Edsel. The Edsel was my parent's first brand new car. Dad had purchased the '57 Ford Country Sedan the year before, from a local used car lot, for the sum of $2,495 cash.

Noon, on Saturday, all the gear was loaded into the new wagon, and we drove the Edsel away from the dealer, Huffman Motors in Aberdeen, to the beach to finish the weekend of clam digging. Mom was the first to drive the new car. The two lane road was clogged with traffic coming back from the beach. Clam digging was over for the day. The direction to the beach was deserted, except for us. I was in the back seat, leaning on the back of the front seat watching over the driver's left shoulder (my favorite position). I was watching the solid line of cars coming at us, and saw the nose of a car pointing out from our side of the road waiting for an opening in traffic. The driver did not see us and jumped out in front of us. Mom swerved the Edsel across the centerline and back avoiding both the car that had pulled out in front of us and all the oncoming traffic. Dad said that he could not have done this. Mom swerved the car so violently, I ended up on the floor in the rear seat with my brother Vern on top of me. Dad always maintained that the Edsel came up on two wheels. The car had 15 miles on it. Dad drove the rest of the way to our camping spot.

During the next four years, until I left home, the Edsel was our primary transportation. When the family went to the beach or the mountains, the wagon was the mode of transport. "Mom's car," a '48 Chevrolet that they had purchased in 1949, was just that, mom's car (another sto-

The award-winning 1959 Edsel Villager station wagon restored by Russ Waterhouse. He recently sold this Edsel but owns nine others, including a 1958 Roundup two-door wagon.

ry). The Edsel took the family everywhere and if my brother or I needed sleep on the road, the wagon was a necessity. That car was my shelter many nights during camping and fishing trips.

After I learned to drive, in late 1961, with expert instruction from dad, including his aforementioned bad habits around "slow pokes," the insurance issue was a problem. Well, to my parents it was not a problem: No insurance, no driving, no problem. After long hours at my part-time, $1.25 per hour position as a "box boy" at a local grocery store, I was able at last to pay the $35 per month for insurance. However, in 1961, driving an Edsel was socially destructive for someone in high school. No one wanted to be seen in a "loser," which the Edsel marque now implied. I found out that I could not pick up a date in a station wagon anyway. Would you let your daughter go out with a kid in a station wagon? Especially an Edsel? I decided to buy my own car. I purchased a '55 Chevrolet hardtop. Chevrolet was more "in."

My social life improved, my driving record did not. In 1963, I graduated from high school and that fall went into the Air Force. It was shortly thereafter that the Edsel wagon became a camping trailer tow vehicle. In the summers, mom, dad and little brother Vern would travel all around the Pacific Northwest. In the fall and winters, to the beach for more clam digging.

Dad wrecked the front two times in the 19 years he owned the Edsel. The second time, in 1972, the body shop installed new grillework and bumpers. "The last ones in Washington state," he was told by the body shop owner. Although the Edsel had been replaced in 1970 by a new Ford three-quarter ton pickup as a trailer tow rig, the wagon was still dad's pride and joy.

Dad used the Edsel for his daily 30-mile round-trip commute to work and for errand running. In 1973, he installed a rebuilt engine and the second rebuilt transmission. Trailer towing had taken its toll.

By 1978, the old wagon was showing its age, and even though dad maintained the mechanics as if it were to last forever, the body could no longer endure the elements. Mom had always kept covers on the seats, at least after the first two weeks when Vern managed to get chewing gum stuck on the back seat. In 1978, dad finally parked the Edsel in a corner of the yard and bought a new Granada. It was worth nothing as a trade-in, and the dealer did not want the Edsel.

In 1979, I had two sons of my own, seven and nine years of age. Both my wife and I worked and drove "econoboxes," but we needed a family car that all of us could fit in at once. I thought about refurbishing a large American car to use as a family car for weekend trips as we did when I was a youngster. The Edsel came to mind, and I went to take a serious look.

The Villager showed its 148,000 miles. Its sparkling white paint was now faded and dull, that is the parts that still had paint. Mold, surface rust, and moss were creeping over it like a huge cloud of doom. Deep rust was showing along the bottom of the front fenders, as well as on both the rear fenders. The windshield had a crack that rivaled the Grand Canyon and the tailgate and rear trim were damaged from a trailer towing inci-

dent. The Edsel had seen many, too many, tight parking spaces. But, the seats still had covers, the rest of the blue interior still looked good and the grille still had sparkle. Dad poured a little gas into the carburetor, hooked jumper cables from his pickup to the lifeless Edsel battery and turned the key. After a couple of turns the engine sprang to life.

I decided then and there that the car would be the one for my family. Naturally, my wife had strong reservations about the entire project. Dad was going to give me the car, but Vern told him to make me buy it, "So I will appreciate it more." (I am still looking for a way to get even for that.) The Edsel cost me $200 and I drove it home.

During the following two years of total restoration, it became a project of perfection. I added factory options such as power steering, power brakes, electric wipers, backup lights, luggage rack, and whitewall tires. The bumpers, door handles, luggage rack and mirrors were rechromed. All the stainless trim was repaired and polished. I did all the body, paint and mechanical work myself. The paint was as the factory had intended, Snow White with a diamond luster finish. The windshield was replaced.

In 1981, I joined the Edsel Owners Club and took it to its first show. That's when I learned of "correct" hose clamps, spark plug wires, natural finished bolts, plated bolts, formed wire terminals, and all the little details of a correctly finished restoration. I had put so much time, effort and money into the restoration, I could not use it as the family car I had once intended. We bought a camper instead.

Over the next 12 years, and with all corrections made, I won over 25 trophies with that Edsel, three of which were "Best of Show." I always drove the car to shows and, not surprisingly, it took the trips well. For a ten year period, I became obsessed with car shows. The Villager was often the only Edsel to be seen outside Edsel club functions and I got several trophies. My life actually revolved around cars and car shows. We made two trips to Southern California from my home near Seattle to attend car club shows and other car club functions.

As with all of us, my lifestyle changed. I found that I no longer had the time or energy to maintain a show car. I needed space in the garage for another project. I could not bring myself to use the car as a daily driver because of the pedestal on which I had placed the car. This meant that the Edsel Villager must be sold. No one in the family wanted the old girl, even though it was still in very good show condition.

In 1995, while attending a club function in the San Francisco Bay area I advertised the Edsel Villager wagon for sale in a local newspaper. It was bought by a collector in California. Now, somewhere in the Bay area, the Edsel sits in storage. Its custom blue cover that I had purchased ten years earlier still protecting the paint. On special occasions the proud new owner, Joe, takes it out for a jaunt down the road again. Fortunately, Joe does keep in touch with me about his experiences with the car. He is enjoying the Edsel.

Am I still an Edsel nut? Well ... yes. I own nine Edsels. I will gladly take you for a ride in my '58 Edsel Roundup (Edsel's only two-door station wagon).

Muddy Monster Chicken Wagon

by Michael Petti
Colonia, New Jersey

A recent television advertisement for a 4x4 made me realize that I was not alone. The theme of the TV commercial has shown either a little boy or girl playing in mud. It fast forwards to the present. They are now adults splashing their vehicles in and out of mud holes. I was the same way as a kid, and did the same thing as a teenager with a station wagon. But, instead of getting in and out of the mud hole, I sank!

In 1966, I was working after school delivering chicken dinners for a local franchise of a national chain. One of the cars I drove was a 1965 Plymouth Valiant station wagon that had a plastic chicken on the roof.

Although I was working, I always felt I was cruising. After all, a one-year-old car is spanking new to a teenager. With the tailgate window rolled down, that wagon became a convertible to me. The fast food chicken chain advertised heavily on all the top 40 rock and roll radio stations. Whenever I stopped for a red light, people never wanted to drag race. Instead, they turned up the volume on their radios to let me know that the ad was playing. I would laugh and give them the thumbs-up in approval.

As a teenager, I loved station wagons, and felt the "chicken" Valiant was mine. I know teenagers are not supposed to like station wagons. Even my dad hated them. He thought they were ugly and noisy. This was the 1960s and the slogan was, "Don't trust anyone over 30." Maybe my love of station wagons, such as the delivery car, was my independence from my dad, as well as a social protest!

Anyway, it was the day before Halloween. I took a short cut through a deserted dirt road. This road was on the border of three towns and each municipality ignored its upkeep. Each mayor must have thought, "Let the other guy fix it." On one side of the road was a lake and on the other side was a cemetery.

It seemed that no one used this road except for me. It was a shortcut to two deliveries that were miles apart. My boss stuck me with the potato-shaped 1958 Rambler American two-door sedan to drive, but it did not get stuck in the mud. Maybe it was because of the American's 15-inch wheels. The mud jolted that car, and I was tossed all around. It was like riding in a rodeo. It was more fun than a roller coaster. I had to go back for more, which I did the next day.

It was Halloween. The time for tricks or treats. Since two deliveries were on opposite sides of the franchise's sales territory, I justified to myself the need to take the dirt road again. It was a treat. What joy racing the Valiant wagon through the mud. I made it through four mud holes, but not the fifth one. The Valiant's 13-inch wheels were no match for this hole. The rest of Halloween was a trick.

Every technique I used when I became stuck in snow or on ice did not work to get out of this mud hole. I walked back to the main road. Since it was Halloween people had their porch lights on anticipating children knocking on their doors for candy. I was able to borrow a shovel at the first house I approached. The more I dug, the faster the mud slid back into the hole. At the same time, the front end of the Valiant was sinking deeper. When the mud reached the front bumper, I knew the wagon had to be towed out.

Exhausted, I rested for a few minutes before walking back to the house where I got the shovel. In the cemetery was a group of pre-teenagers dressed in costumes. They must have dared each other to walk through the graveyard. I was leaning against a tombstone when they saw me. They screamed and ran. As a reflex reaction, I screamed. I ran to reassure them it was all right, but this scared them even more.

They must have thought I was a bogeyman. My clothes were all mud stained. These kids could have thought my clothes were blood stained.

The cemetery was hilly. As I turned around I could not see the wagon. I did see the plastic chicken illuminated by the moonlight. If I was in the car spinning back and forth, these Halloweeners would have thought it was a monster chicken wobbling.

I returned the shovel and asked the home owners to telephone my boss. He arrived with two other delivery guys on duty that night. At worst, I thought I would be fired. At best, yelled at for such stupidity. Instead, my boss was glad I was not in an accident. He even praised me for trying to save some mileage with the shortcut!

Still, I was humiliated. The boss hooked a chain from the Valiant onto the Rambler American. The much-despised Rambler towed the much-beloved Valiant wagon out of the mud hole effortlessly. What a trick!

From Collector Car to Daily Driver

by James Jaeger
Buffalo, Minnesota

It all started one evening when my wife, Mary, and I went to preview the cars in a local antique car auction. We have both had an interest in antique cars for many years, both owning 1956 Buicks, and went to the auction to see the cars, check on price trends and to watch people. As we were looking over the field of cars to pass over the auction block, Mary spotted a 1955 Buick Special four-door and got the idea it would make an interesting car to drive to work.

As I looked over the car, Mary continued looking for other possible candidates to be a daily driver. She soon came across a 1961 Corvair 700 Lakewood station wagon licensed as a collector car. The car really caught her eye.

The auction was not until the next day so Mary started to research a price she was willing to pay for the 1955 Buick. The Corvair wagon remained in the back of her mind. I knew nothing about Corvairs and was much more in favor of the Buick since we had a lot of spare parts and knowledge of the car's mechanics. Mary settled on a price she was willing to pay for the Buick and we were off to the auction.

The Buick went far above what Mary wanted to pay. As we continued to watch cars cross the block the Corvair appeared in the doorway. When the Corvair was on the block I soon noticed the auctioneer was looking in our direction and then noticed our bidding number was

James and Mary Jaeger's 1961 Corvair 700 Lakewood station wagon. This car is a daily driver for most of the year.

181

The Corvair 700 Lakewood station wagon owned by James and Mary Jaeger is parked with its garage mates, a 1993 Buick Roadmaster wagon (right) and a 1956 Buick Century wagon, which is another story.

in motion. After a spirited bidding session the car was ours. I then realized we were 50 miles from home and had just purchased a car neither of us understood.

We paid for the little car and went to pick up our new acquisition. The car looked solid and ran when Mary hit the starter. With fingers crossed we headed home with the little car smoking and wobbling as Mary learned to manage a rear engine car.

Mary started to drive the car to work. We joined the local and national Corvair clubs and started the process of learning about the car Ralph Nader said was unsafe at any speed. Our first long excursion was to the local Corvair chapter club meeting. This involved 26 miles of strange noises. When we arrived we discovered the brakes on one of the rear wheels was stuck and we had a hot wheel. The club members provided a lot of advice

on where to get parts and who understood Corvairs. We started to sort out the little car and learned more of its history. We would later learn the car's previous owner lived close to our home. It had been in the same family since new. It was stored most of the year and driven only when one of the family members visited from Europe. This explained the German radio.

We have now owned and worked on the little Corvair for three years. It is Mary's daily driver every year until the snow begins to fly. Since the Lakewood wagon was only made in 1961, the car attracted a lot of attention and we have younger people asking what kind of car it is. Mary spends a lot of time hearing stories about Corvairs from people who approach her in parking lots. Most people loved their Corvairs. Possibly Ralph Nader killed a very good and economical car.

From Junker To Show Car

by James Jaeger
Buffalo, Minnesota

My wife Mary's beloved 1956 Buick Century Estate Wagon is not stock, but we tried to keep it as original in appearance as possible while adding updated mechanics and creature comforts. We did this to preserve a car of limited production, as only 8,094 were made.

It was a warm summer day when Mary came home and said she was sure she had just seen a station wagon that looked the same as "Sherman" our 1956 Buick Super sedan. She described it as pink, white, black and a lot of rust, but was sure it was a 1956 Buick wagon. I had never seen a 1956 Buick wagon and was interested in

tracking it down. The next day we came across the wagon in our local shopping center. She was correct, it was a 1956 Buick wagon with all those colors and a whole bunch of rust and the owner's name carved in the hood.

As it turned out, the car belonged to one of our children's friends. In secret, I had the children negotiate for the car as a wedding anniversary gift. For $150 the 1956 Buick Century wagon joined our family. It was a mess. Everything was wrong with the car and work progressed slowly until winter set in. The car was then moved to winter storage on a friend's farm. The project was placed on the back burner as other things took priority until we were notified that the farm was sold. A decision had to be made about what to do with the wagon.

Mary wanted a vacation car that she felt comfortable driving so we decided to update the wagon with modern running gear and preserve the original design of the body. We located a talented young craftsman to work on the car. We wanted to use all Buick parts in creating the modified Century wagon. It was determined we would leave the interior and exterior stock. The car would be powered by a Buick 455-cid engine with a turbo 400 transmission. A 1970 Buick wagon was selected as the engine donor. We later learned the engine was not original to the car and was found to be a Buick Gran Sport Stage One engine!

For steering, our craftsman recommended we use an AMC Pacer rack and pinion unit. It was then that I found out the AMC Pacer was a 5,000 pound car. The Pacer steering was almost a bolt-on to the original 1956 frame.

For the rear end our first choice was a 1970 Skylark, but it was too wide. A 1964 LeSabre was found to fit. Creature comforts such as cruise control and air conditioning were added to the plan. The interior was planned to be close to the factory specifications, but going with the black and white just did not seem to fit with the exterior colors. Instead, the interior was done in coral, white and black to match the exterior.

With the addition of the 455 engine in the lightweight Century, the car is a sleeper. Mary enjoys surprising many motorists by blowing their doors off after they point and make fun of the old car. The car responds the same as any 1970 Gran Sport with a Stage One engine. Since completion, Mary and I have taken the car on a number of vacation trips and it has been to many Buick Club of America regional and national shows in the Midwest. Because of the colors, the car has become well known as "Petunia" after the cartoon character.

James and Mary Jaeger's pair of Buick station wagons, a 1956 Century Estate Wagon and a 1993 Roadmaster. The Century can almost be considered a full-tilt racing machine with its 455-cid Stage One powerplant.

You Don't Bring Me Flowers, Anymore

by William H. Ursprung, Jr.
Palmyra, Pennsylvania

The original purchase of my 1957 Ford Del Rio Ranch Wagon (powered by the Thunderbird 292-cid V-8) was made on Dec. 24, 1956. The following list shows the price of each option:

The wagon was used as a backup delivery for a local florist for 10 years. It was stored from 1968 until 1986. The Del Rio now has 83,700 miles on it. It has been repainted once and the interior seats and headliner have new old stock fabric.

A former florist delivery vehicle, William Ursprung, Jr. is the second owner of this 1957 Ford Del Rio Ranch Wagon. The car was repainted and has new old stock headliner and seat covering, otherwise the Ford is original with fewer than 85,000 miles on it.

1957 Ford Del Rio Ranch Wagon

Raven Black—$2,780.00
Magic Air Heater—$69.00
Undercoating—$5.00
Wheel Covers—$20.00
Gold Anodized Molding—$15.00
Backup Lights—$9.00
7.50 x 14 four-ply whitewall tires—$34.00
Pennsylvania Sales Tax—$66.00
Total with License & Title Fee—$3,033.00

Lone Survivor?

by Gary Engel/Dan Walsh
South Sioux City, Nebraska

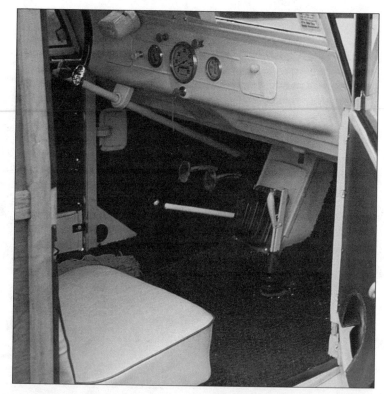

We found a 1941 Crosley "woodie" station wagon in 1978 in an abandoned warehouse. Hearing of a small wooden car inside the warehouse, we were quite curious.

We were eventually able to get inside the warehouse to see the car. It appeared to be leaning against a pole. It had a four-cylinder engine in it. We bought the car, and later located a two-cylinder engine in Florida. Many other parts were obtained in five different states.

We have several nice restored and original cars of the same era, but the Crosley is always a favorite at the car shows, and with others who see our collection.

We believe this 1941 Crosley "Covered Wagon" is the lone survivor.

Different views of the interior show the pristine condition of this restored Crosley. This car sold for less than $500 new, and due to its low production owners Gary Engel and Dan Walsh wonder if their 1941 Crosley wagon is the only survivor.

With its fabric roof, the 1941 Crosley "woodie" was called a Covered Wagon. This model was rescued from an abandoned warehouse and restored by Gary Engel and Dan Walsh.

A True "Sleeper"

George Eichinger of Allegan, Mich., made a camper top on his 1957 Plymouth Sport Suburban six-passenger station wagon. The car is equipped with a 318-cid V-8 engine, automatic transmission, and power steering. Paint is white with gold trim. The window in the tailgate rolls down. The 5 x 9-foot camper top is a wooden frame covered with aluminum resting on a gutter rail. The cover is also a wooden frame covered with aluminum, which is held up with a four-foot pipe. Also included is a brown canvas cover on the sides with screen windows on the front and each side and a zipper on the back. Eichinger's sons sleep on top (Ron is pictured). When the cover is in the down position, all luggage and camping gear are inside.

The K9 Car

by Stephen Tuma
Grand Ledge, Michigan

Dog Jason's "woofer wagon" was built on Feb. 20, 1986, because of one man's love of road trips with his best friend and a mistake by Ford Motor Co.

In 1983, Jason and Steve Tuma, his human friend and constant companion, began twice yearly vacations from Michigan (where they administered a small county parks system) to the Dakotas and then North Carolina to visit with parents and their dog, Miss Duchess.

"I learned a lot about road travel with Jason in our car, at the time a 1979 Pontiac LeMans four-door sedan," Tuma said.

One lesson was Jason's need for more stretching space while traveling between favorite state and county parks along the way. Tuma tried to solve this challenge by purchasing a new Ford LTD station wagon in August of 1985. With the rear seat down the car became a rolling kennel. Jason was ecstatic! Tuma was too, until a week later, he discovered thousands of dimples in the paint on the car's hood and top. Tuma demanded a new car. Ford Motor Co. officials said they would sand down the paint to remove the dimples. In chess, this is called a stalemate.

Ford's stalemate solver, The Consumer's Board of Appeals, was contacted. In December of 1985 (Friday the 13th to be exact), the board told "The Company" to make Tuma and Jason happy. The result is Jason's "K9 Car," special ordered in January of 1986.

Silver metallic with a clove brown interior, the LTD Crown Victoria station wagon has ten options: air conditioning, tinted glass, power windows, power front seat, tilt steering wheel, cruise control, right-hand remote mirror, interval windshield wipers, bumper rub strips, and a conventional spare tire.

The "K9 Car" is an excellent road machine turning long stretches of interstate travel into living room comfort. The storage area under the load floor easily handles all luggage and gear necessary for extended travel, save for the food and water cooler left handy for cool drinks and treats after walking nature trails.

Jason thoroughly enjoyed vacation travel in the "K9 Car." Tragedy struck after the spring 1994 trip, however, when he died at home with Tuma and Miss Kitty by his side. The wagon, with 127,000 miles on it, is still like new and factory original except for replacement items such as tires, spark plugs, and filters. Since November of 1986, the Ford has always been garaged and covered unless being driven on nice summer days or vacation.

Currently, Collie dog Jackson (a household resident since the spring of 1995) and Tuma still take one of their two annual vacation trips in the "K9 Car." On both trips they equally enjoy visiting favorite state and county parks along the way. Quite frankly, however, they enjoy traveling more in the wagon than their new Explorer. The difference is simple: The station wagon was built as a road car while the Explorer, an excellent unit in its own right, is a sport utility.

Stephen Tuma's 1986 Ford LTD Crown Victoria station wagon, which he calls the "K9 Car" for obvious reasons. That's "Jackson" chowing down at a roadside park.

Wide World Of Wagons:
Clubs, Collectibles, Concept Cars and Something Called "The Intergalactic Crunch-off"

www.wagon.com or How I found my woodie while surfin' the 'Net

Web sites. Search engines. Home pages. Links. These are all terms that need to be understood to successfully navigate the Internet via a personal computer. To the novice 'Net user, this can be somewhat intimidating, but if that novice is also a station wagon enthusiast it's definitely worth learning the ways of the www.world. While there remains no subject that cannot be explored in some fashion on the Internet, station wagons, while a small niche in the overall automotive big picture, have decent representation on the 'Net.

Keying in the word station wagon in any of the Internet-access search engines or specifically keying in www.stationwagon.com will access a home page created and copyrighted by station wagon enthusiast Steve Manning of Maryland. Manning has titled his creation "The Home of the American Station Wagon." The page's subtitle leaves no doubt as to Manning's allegiance to the extinct station wagon: "Dedicated to preserving information about the classic station wagon ... which has almost been replaced by the *evil* minivan."

Manning's home page offers diverse information about station wagons as well as links to other wagon-related web sites. This "grocery list" of links includes several that are nothing more than an individual's web site devoted to his or her favorite station wagon. These usually include a photo of the favorite wagon, factory statis-

tics about that particular wagon and, if you're lucky, maybe a poem or personal story written about the dream machine. Particular station wagons listed recently as web site subjects included: a 1953 Buick Roadmaster Estate Wagon, 1954 Nash Rambler Cross Country, a prototype 1959 Imperial two-door wagon discovered in Sweden, 1961 Chevrolet Corvair Lakewood and 1962 Monza (rare wagon model), 1966 Chevy Impala, 1968 Plymouth Sport Suburban (Manning's contribution) and 1975 Ford LTD.

If you're looking for something more altruistic than station wagon statistics and poetry, why not "Help Save The Whales" by calling up the web site devoted to the American Station Wagon Owners Association. This club, written about elsewhere in this book, is devoted to the promotion and preservation of station wagons. The club's home page offers membership information and convention dates and locations. This club has been active for only a short period of time, but has already become the driving force for station wagon owners in North America. By the way, "Help Save The Whales" is the club's motto!

One of the most useful web sites devoted to station wagons is the "In Search Of ..." site. Similar to classified "want" ads, persons interested in locating the wagon of their dreams list their needs (year, marque, model, color,

Steve Manning's 1968 Plymouth Sport Suburban station wagon, with aftermarket wheels, which is one of many wagons rhapsodized about on the Internet.

accessories desired, etc.) as well as their personal web site addresses. No "for sale" ads are accepted, only want ads. The site is operated by Manning, who handles the organizing and updating of the ads as well as sending and receiving e-mail to and from the "wagon wanters" interested in posting an ad.

While mainstream station wagon subjects such as woodies and Nomads have their place on Manning's home page, there is also room for the offbeat. This is where the (missing?) link to Wagons of Steel web site comes in. This site is a promotional page devoted to alerting station wagon enthusiasts to the fact that Wagons of Steel magazine (better known as a "zine") has been self-published since 1991 by Chris Barnes (better known as Gaffo F. Jones) of Vashon, Wash. This "zine" contains an eclectic mix of fact, fiction and fantasy concerning the station wagon. An example of the offbeat nature of this publication comes in the form of a letter to the editor in issue #5 (pictured):

"Dear Wagons of Steel, While cleaning up my latest station wagon I found the carcass of a very large lizard-like creature under the spare tire. I fear that it may be an endangered species. What should I do"? (signed) RT, Oakland, OR

"Dear RT, Whatever danger the lizard was in is over now because it's dead. I recommend that you put it on the barby and call it chicken."

Ole' Gaffo is a screenprinter by trade, so *Wagons of Steel* is chocked full of interesting, often bizarre artwork depicting station wagons, and it's definitely a publication that has to be read to be believed!

With the Internet growing at an almost limitless pace, the station wagon web site offerings are also bound to increase. Even the manufacturers are using the Internet to promote new wagon models (at least what passes for a station wagon today!), with Audi listing a web site to hawk its wares.

Searching (or surfin') the 'Net for station wagon information is an interesting journey into both the history and current status of wagons as well as offering some entertaining side trips. Boot up your PC, and enjoy the ride!

Wagons of Steel **magazine, since 1991 devoted to anything and everything station wagon.**

Wagon Worship

There is a bit of irony in the fact that the American Station Wagon Owners Association's first annual convention was held in Indianapolis. At the mention of this most famous of Hoosier cities the first thing that comes to mind is the Memorial Classic 500-mile race featuring single-seat open wheel race cars with needle-nose aerodynamics. But on a steamy day in July of 1997, the city of speed was the gathering point for vehicles known for their multi-passenger seating and aerodynamics akin to a brick.

That this gathering took place at all was basically the work of one man, Indianapolis resident Ken McDaniel, founder of the American Station Wagon Owners Association (ASWOA). It was also at this outing that, maybe, for the first time, McDaniel could see light at the end of the tailgate as far as his long range plan for ASWOA was concerned. That plan, more mission-like in intensity, is to elevate awareness among car enthusiasts of the station wagon's rightful place alongside the sportier models that previously have garnered most of the attention as desirable collector cars.

"It is my hope that station wagons will become as much an accepted part of the old car hobby as convertibles and hardtops. Station wagons are slowly disappearing and will be gone unless some are saved today," McDaniel emphasized.

His devotion to the long roofs stems from a childhood of being ferried about in a long line of station wagons, including a 1966 Buick Special and 1968 Buick Sport Wagon. "We always had a wagon," stressed McDaniel. Even now he owns and regularly drives the 1977 Chevrolet Malibu Classic station wagon purchased new by his parents.

Looking admiringly at the wine-colored Chevy parked on the showgrounds at the ASWOA convention, McDaniel said, "My wagon is nothing special. But I learned to drive in it, we took family vacations in it, I had my first date in it ... that's why it's special to me!"

McDaniel is the antithesis of the stereotypical show promoter/club "spark plug." Calm and reserved in speech, his "low profile" demeanor allows the spotlight

Ken McDaniel of Indianapolis is president of American Station Wagon Owners Association (ASWOA). His 1977 Chevrolet Malibu Classic station wagon was formerly owned by his parents, and he has fond memories of family vacations, his first date and learning to drive in this car. The Chevy's license plates promote McDaniel's major dislike of minivans.

to shine on the station wagons he so strongly believes have gotten the car hobby's back seat treatment.

"You go to a lot of [car] shows and people laugh at wagon owners," laments McDaniel. He is not one to take that kind of attitude with his tailgate lying down.

McDaniel is devoted to making a go of the ASWOA. Since the club's inception in mid-1996, he and his wife Natalie have worked hard to publish a monthly newsletter appropriately titled *From The Tailgate*. This club pub includes the usual fare such as letters to the editor, accounts of members' wagons, club-related news and, as a bonus, several pages of color photos of ASWOA members' station wagons. The McDaniels also performed all the organizational chores for the aforementioned first annual ASWOA convention, which had a decent turnout for a first-time event.

"Ten percent of our members are here [at the convention]," McDaniel beamed. He added, "For a stand alone [event] with a one-year-old club, ten percent turnout is fantastic."

Left unsaid in McDaniel's member attendance tally is the fact that several non-ASWOA members brought station wagons to the convention. With McDaniel's zeal to "grow" the membership ranks of the club, it is a good bet that these wagon owners left the gathering with ASWOA membership cards in their wallets.

> "It is my hope that station wagons will become as much an accepted part of the old car hobby as convertibles and hardtops. Station wagons are slowly disappearing and will be gone unless some are saved today".
>
> *Ken McDaniel, president*
> **American Station Wagon Owners Assoc.**

The first annual ASWOA convention held in July of 1997 in Indianapolis was definitely a family affair. Victoria Englin of Aurora, Ill., dusts her uncle Doug's 1960 Chevy Nomad prior to the judging portion of the car show. She must have done a good job as the Nomad won the ASWOA "Grand Champion" award at the convention.

While it may have taken some time to count heads at the ASWOA gathering, it was easy to count the trailers used to transport the approximately 30 station wagons exhibited at the event. None. *Nada.* Zero. "All of the cars were driven to the show," McDaniel boasted. The impact of that statement cannot be fully appreciated until the points of origin of the participants are revealed. Attendees came to Indianapolis from as far away as Connecticut, Iowa, Maryland, Ohio and Pennsylvania.

Even the fact that the bulk of the convention attendees came from the states of Indiana, Michigan and Illinois, this in itself is interesting, according to McDaniel. These states tend to have harsh climates and the station wagon survival rate in these cold weather climes is abysmal at best. Road salt-induced rust and slippery road condition-induced accidents as well as the county fair-season demolition derbies have prematurely sent many a fine wagon to the salvage yards. That a good number of ASWOA members and show-attending station wagons are based in the Midwest (Midworst?) is cause for celebration and a rousing chant of the ASWOA motto: "Help Save the Whales!"

ASWOA's second annual convention is locked in. The club has a healthy, growing membership. With that, instead of the people at the car shows looking down on the owners of station wagons, it may be Ken McDaniel and the American Station Wagon Owners Association that will be getting the last laugh.

One of several interesting station wagons at the ASWOA convention was this 1976 Cadillac Castilian conversion. Termed a "Sports Wagon," the Castilian features a sunroof, a forward-angled C pillar that sweeps up and over the roof, and a raked rear window/liftgate with attached air deflector.

This pristine 1966 Ford Ranch Wagon owned by Steve and Tammy Walker of Waterloo, Iowa, won the ASWOA "Best Daily Driver" award at the convention. And, yes, the car is as clean inside as it is outside.

Gerald and Ann Seacat of Greenwood, Ind., are the proud owners of this original 1958 Plymouth Custom Suburban station wagon. As evidenced by these photos, the Seacat's meticulous care of their Plymouth paid off with it winning the ASWOA "Best Original Unrestored" award at the convention.

The Indianapolis Embassy Suites North hotel hosted the American Station Wagon Owners Association first annual convention in 1997. The wagons at the show, all driven to the event, ranged from a 1954 Nash Rambler Greenbrier to a 1985 Chevrolet Caprice.

American Station Wagon Owners Association
6110 Bethesda Way
Indianapolis, IN 46254-5060
(317)291-0321

Other station wagon-related clubs and/or publications

Chevrolet Nomad Association (1955-1957)
publication: *The Nomad Post*
2537 S. 87th Ave.
Omaha, NE 68124

National Woodie Club
publication: *Woodie Times*
3028 South St.
Lincoln, NE 68502

publication: *Wagons of Steel*
P.O. Box 1435
Vashon, WA 98070

Wrecking Yard Wagons

As the saying goes, "It doesn't get any better than this" when it comes to a car enthusiast's visit to a salvage yard. Call them wrecking yards, junkyards or a slice of heaven on earth, nowhere else can the "thrill of the hunt" be so exciting.

Salvage yards dot the landscape of America. Most are filled with modern "iron," but many yards exist that are stocked with the treasures of the past. It is in these treasure-troves that station wagons that plied the highways of postwar America languish under the harsh summer sun and frigid winter snows. The wood-bodied wagons of the 1930s and early-1940s have all but returned to the earth. However, the steel-bodied wagons produced after the "woodie" era can still be found, although yards in drier, warmer climates such as the southwest U.S. probably have more of the intact mid-1940s to 1960s examples.

Many of these station wagons rusting in peace still have salvageable parts that could complete another wagon restoration project. It is also still possible to find solid, complete station wagons of the past that were driven into a yard and parked. Most cars in salvage yards suffer from both the assault of nature and abuse of vandals who enjoy smashing windows and hammering on sheet metal just for "kicks." To find one of these undamaged and complete wagons is becoming ever more difficult, but, again, the "thrill of the hunt" can often have a happy ending.

Obscured by overgrown branches, this 1955 Chrysler New Yorker Town & Country station wagon still had many usable grille and trim pieces. Only 1,036 of these New Yorkers were built, so a rare model such as this, even in extremely rough condition, might be worth restoring.

This 1955 Pontiac Chieftain 870 station wagon appears to have been a car that was driven into the salvage yard and parked. Aside from missing its headlight trim rings and some broken windows, the car was amazingly complete right down to its hubcaps.

Although the rocker panels showed plenty of rust-through, this 1957 Oldsmobile 88 Fiesta station wagon was a rare and desirable hardtop model. Only 5,767 of these beauties were built. Parked in front of the Fiesta hardtop wagon was its B-pillared counterpart, called the Fiesta "Sedan" to distinguish it from the hardtop 88.

Rusty in all the wrong places, this 1957 Mercury Commuter two-door station wagon would still have yielded many good parts, especially the intact wraparound quarter glass and solid "coupe-style" doors. This six-passenger Commuter had a small production run of 4,885 and was one of Mercury's Nomad/Safari fighters.

Introduced into the 1963 Ford Fairlane 500 station wagon line was this Squire model, with only 7,983 produced. Available with either six-cylinder or V-8 power, this wagon was badged as having the Challenger 260-cid V-8. Remnants of an optional luggage rack remained on the Squire's roof.

Retaining its "horse collar" grillework, this 1958 Edsel Bermuda station wagon was the top-line Edsel wagon in its introductory year. Its simulated wood trim also appeared to be in good shape. Only 892 of these Edsel wagons were built.

In its final year of production in 1960, Edsel offered only the Villager line of station wagons in six- and nine-passenger configurations. Production totaled a paltry 216 and 59, respectively. This Villager appeared nearly complete and solid. It was a plumbing contractor's work vehicle and probably saw rough use hauling tools and hardware.

Wagons Workin' on the Railroad

(Photos and information courtesy of Carroll Collins and Fairmont Tamper, Harsco Corp.)

The first Fairmont® HY-RAIL® unit was shipped in July of 1949. Early units were primarily based on the Willys-Overland Jeep chassis with a Fairmont-built body. These work vehicles were available in several configurations, primarily as transportation for section gang crews.

In the mid-1950s, as the HY-RAIL unit was further refined, the need for a comfortable, luxury vehicle from which railroad management officials could "inspect" the line was desired. At the time, railroads generally required a management official to inspect all of its track miles at least once a year. This was usually done from one of the railroad's business cars pulled at the rear of a train or even by a special inspection train. A luxury class road/rail vehicle would be ideal for the job allowing the inspector to stop at will or get off the track after covering a specific area and proceed via highway to the next location.

Enter the HY-RAIL guide wheel equipped station wagon. With their heavy-duty frame on chassis construction, load-carrying suspension and rigid bodies, the station wagon was an ideal vehicle for the job. Beginning in 1954, Pontiac was the vehicle of choice, with a large number being equipped until Pontiac introduced its famous "wide track" design in the early 1960s. The wide track suspension design made the vehicle's tread width too wide to fit on the 56-1/2 inch track gauge and the Pontiac was eliminated from road/rail use.

Station wagons from General Motors, Ford and the Chrysler lines were all used as inspection vehicles throughout the late 1950s, 1960s and the early 1970s. When the energy crunch of the 1970s brought downsizing and unibody construction, the role of the station wagon in road/rail service was over. With station wagons from the Big Three no longer suitable for conversion, railroads turned for a short time to the wagons from Checker and American Motors.

In the mid-1970s, a new type of station wagon became the mainstay for track inspection transportation. Chevrolet/GMC Suburbans and Jeep Wagoneers with rugged truck-type frames and the availability of four-wheel-drive virtually eliminated the passenger car wagons and sedans from road/rail service.

Today, sport utility vehicles from most vehicle manufacturers continue the important job of providing reliable transportation for the inspectors who ensure that the railways of the world are safe for trains.

1955 Pontiac Chieftain Deluxe 870 station wagon fitted with Fairmont HY-RAIL wheels. Note the factory-option wide whitewall tires. This three-seat Chieftain also had vent windows ("ventipanes") in the front and rear glass. (Photo courtesy Fairmont Tamper, Harsco Corp.)

1963 Buick LeSabre station wagon fitted with Fairmont HY-RAIL wheels. That's a dealer sticker still attached to this new car's window. Note the "scrub pads" out front of the rail wheels to clean debris off the tracks that might otherwise cause a derailment. Also, this Buick is equipped with dual spotlights for possible use in nighttime track inspection duties. (Photo courtesy Fairmont Tamper, Harsco Corp.)

1963 Checker Marathon station wagon fitted with Fairmont HY-RAIL wheels. The Checker's original bumpers were not re-installed on the vehicle after the HY-RAIL system was installed. Those are Goodyear snow tires mounted on the rear. Note the factory-option roof rack. (Photo courtesy Fairmont Tamper, Harsco Corp.)

1960 Mercury Country Cruiser Commuter station wagon fitted with Fairmont HY-RAIL wheels. This wagon featured hardtop styling and wraparound windshield. Note the badge on the front fender that reads: Fairmont HY-RAIL Motor Car. (Photo courtesy Fairmont Tamper, Harsco Corp.)

The Ranch Wagon was Ford's base trim level station wagon for 1961. A dealer sticker is visible in the window as is a rear license plate, D1708-1, which is a Fairmont-use plate issued by the Minnesota Dept. of Motor Vehicles to allow the car to be test-driven. (Photo courtesy Fairmont Tamper, Harsco Corp.)

Posed on a brick street with its HY-RAIL wheels retracted, this 1964 Ford Country Sedan also is badged as a Fairmont HY-RAIL Motor Car. The "scrub pads" are visible in front of the HY-RAIL wheels. This Ford also does not have its original chrome bumpers re-installed. That same D1708-1 license plate shown on the 1961 Ford appears again on this base level trim station wagon. (Photo courtesy Fairmont Tamper, Harsco Corp.)

Another on-the-road shot of a Fairmont-badged 1964 Chrysler New Yorker Town & Country station wagon with hardtop styling. Again, the Chrysler's original chrome bumpers have not been re-installed, and visible on the front HY-RAIL platform is a double set of spotlights for nighttime track maintenance. (Photo courtesy Fairmont Tamper, Harsco Corp.)

A late-1950s Willys Jeep Utility Wagon fitted with Fairmont HY-RAIL wheels. This two-door "station wagon" carried the Fairmont badge on its front fender and a spare tire in its cargo area. Barely visible is the dealer sticker in the window on the driver's side of the Jeep. It appears that the "arms" attached to the HY-RAIL wheels had to be longer than those on a passenger car station wagon due to the Jeep's higher ground clearance. (Photo courtesy Fairmont Tamper, Harsco Corp.)

1964 Plymouth Savoy station wagon fitted with Fairmont HY-RAIL wheels. This Plymouth has a dealer sticker as well as a warranty sticker in the window. Due to the original chrome bumpers not being re-installed, the directional lights have been moved from their original bumper-mounted location to the ends of the front HY-RAIL platform. A spotlight has also been mounted on the A pillar. This base level Savoy came equipped with a factory-option roof rack. (Photo courtesy Fairmont Tamper, Harsco Corp.)

1961 Chevrolet Parkwood station wagon fitted with Fairmont HY-RAIL wheels. The tires on this Chevy appear to be well worn in contrast to the newness of the car. The Parkwood was trimmed similar to the Bel Air series that year. Again, a dealer sticker is visible in the window. (Photo courtesy Fairmont Tamper, Harsco Corp.)

Station Wagon Collectibles

The wide world of automobilia includes an extensive array of collectibles focusing on the station wagon. It's a good bet that woodies and Nomads are the subjects of much of this auto memorabilia, but the "standard" versions of station wagons also have decent representation as collectible items.

Station wagons are best represented in rolling memorabilia, which is toy cars and plastic model kits or factory promotional models. Most of the toy companies that produce(d) downsized metal cars, including Corgi, Dinky, Matchbox and Tootsietoy, all have versions of station wagons in miniature. Who among car enthusiasts didn't as a child own a coffee can or collector case full of these neat little cars, creating imaginary highways in the sandbox or on the sofa and cruising at "reduced" speed?

The list of station wagons that have achieved increased value among these miniature metal machines is lengthy and includes: from Corgi, a 1959 Plymouth Suburban in stock and mail car versions and 1963 Studebaker Lark Daytona Wagonaire in camera car (cameraman standing in cargo area with car's sliding roof panel open) and "amblewagon" versions; from Dinky, a 1948 Plymouth "woodie," 1958 Nash Rambler in stock and fire chief versions, 1961 Rambler Cross Country and 1965 Rambler Classic; from Matchbox, a 1956 Ford "Customline" (Country Sedan), 1959 Ford "Fairlane" (Country Sedan), 1963 Studebaker Lark Daytona Wagonaire with two or three white plastic figures of hunter and dog(s), 1969 Mercury "Commuter" (Monterey) in stock or oversize (4-3/8 inches long) police version and 1978 Dodge Monaco in either yellow or red fire chief versions; from Tootsietoy, several "generic" versions of prewar "woodie" wagons, 1948 Buick Estate Wagon, 1954 Buick Estate Wagon, 1954 Ford Ranch Wagon (Country Sedan) that also came as a set including a police badge and whistle, 1956 Pontiac Safari, 1959 Ford, 1960 Ford, 1960 Rambler and 1962 Ford, which also came in two additional set versions including either a boat and trailer or a trailer filled with four racing tires.

On a larger scale, tin toys by manufacturers such as Marx also offered versions of station wagons. In the case of Marx, each of the four versions of station wagons produced was a "generic" car. These tin wagons were 6-3/4, 7, 7-1/2 and 11 inches long, respectively. A version of the 6-3/4-inch tin wagon was part of a Marx set issued in 1950 that also included a roadster and a nine-inch metal garage to house the two cars. Japanese toy manufacturers also produced many friction-powered American station wagons in tin including: from ATC (Asahi Toy Co.), a 1962 Ford Country Sedan; from Asakusa, a 1968 Buick Sportwagon; from Bandai, a 1955 Ford Custom Ranch Wagon, 1957 Ford Del Rio Ranch Wagon, 1959 Rambler Cross Country (available in two different sets: one with an accompanying Cabin Cruiser boat and boat trailer and the other with a Shasta travel trailer, or as a five-piece set including the Rambler, boat and trailer and outboard motor, and travel trailer) and 1961 Ford Country Sedan (from the "Automobiles of the World" series); from Haji, a 1958 Edsel Roundup in stock and ambulance versions;

from Ichiko, a 1961 Plymouth Deluxe Suburban "International TV Car" with cameraman and television camera on roof, also available in ambulance version (both battery-powered); from N.K. Toys (Korea), 1961 Rambler Cross Country; from T.N., a 1958 Edsel Roundup; from Yonezawa, a 1950s Jeep station wagon and 1959 Buick; and from makers unknown, a 1954 Buick Estate Wagon (battery-powered), 1959 Ford Ranch Wagon, 1960 Chevrolet and 1965 Ford Country Squire.

In plastic model kits, station wagon kits that have exceeded $100 in value (excellent condition) include: from Hubley, a 1960 Ford Country Squire 4-in-1 kit #154-K, issued in 1960; from Aurora, 1951 Mercury "woodie" from the television series "Mod Squad," kit number unknown, issued in 1969; from Revell, 1957 Ford Country Squire kit #H-1220, issued in 1957; from AMT: George Barris Customized Surf Woodie kit #2166, issued in 1965; 1964 Chevrolet Chevelle Malibu 3-in-1 kit #8744, issued in 1964; 1963 Chevrolet Chevy II Nova with trailer, Craftsman Series kit #08-743, issued in 1963; and, 1960 Chevrolet Nomad (four-door station wagon) Junior Craftsman Series kit #04-740, issued in 1963.

The station wagon has probably been represented most often within the realm of dealer promotionals, or "promos" as these usually 1/25th-scale automobiles are commonly called. Promos were created in several varieties including: pot metal, cast aluminum, die-cast white metal, plastic, banks (with coin slots), promos with friction motors, key-wind motors and coaster versions. Many manufacturers were involved in producing dealer promotionals. The list of metal station wagon promos that have exceeded $100 in value (excellent condition) include: from Al-Toy, 1949 Jeep station wagon of sand cast aluminum (14-1/2 inches long) and from Authenticast, 1959-1963 Jeep station wagon. Plastic station wagon promos valued in excess of $100 (excellent condition) include: from AMT, 1961 Buick Special (non-friction version), 1962 Buick Special, 1963 Chevy II, 1964 Chevy Malibu and 1965 Chevy Malibu; from Hubley, 1960 Ford Country Sedan, 1961 Ford Country Sedan and 1962 Ford Country Sedan; from Johan, 1960 Plymouth Sport Suburban (version with torsion bars), 1964 Rambler Classic and 1965 Rambler Classic; from PMC (Product Miniature Co.), 1950 Plymouth Special Deluxe in 1/20th scale, 1951 Plymouth Special Deluxe in 1/20th scale, 1952 Plymouth Concord in 1/20th scale, 1953 Chevy Handyman in 1/20th scale, 1954 Plymouth Belvedere in stock and ambulance versions, 1955 Ford Country Sedan in stock and Red Cross versions, 1956 Ford Country Sedan in stock and Red Cross versions, 1956 Chevy Bel Air, 1957 Ford Country Sedan, 1958 Ford Country Sedan and 1959 Ford Country Sedan (with "Ford Aire" on tailgate); from SMP (Scale Model Products), 1957 Chevy Bel Air in both plastic and metal chassis versions, 1958 Chevy Nomad (four-door station wagon), 1959 Chevy Nomad (four-door) and 1960 Chevy Nomad (four-door); and from an unknown manufacturer, a 1956 Rambler Cross Country.

How to Live (it up) in a Station Wagon!

One of the more interesting station wagon collectibles is a small softcover book titled *Ford Treasury of Station Wagon Living*. This long-out-of-print book, published in 1957, was put out by the Ford Motor Co. in conjunction with the popular *Ford Times* magazine. The editor's note explaining why the book was published defines the time period perfectly:

This book, we dare say, is the only one of its kind in existence. It is a light-hearted reference book dealing with a gay and relaxed subject—the afternoon picnic or beach party, the weekend outing, the camping vacation....

Later, in the introduction, this invocation continues:

Its object is to aid and comfort the vast and growing army of those who are discovering the merit of the station wagon as a rolling recreation center. ...we think you'll find the book stimulating. Better yet, we think it will be of concrete help to you when you sit down to plan your next family excursion, whether it's a Sunday afternoon picnic or a long camping trip to a strange, far place.

The focus of the book is all the camping, boating, sleeping and field cooking gear available that could be loaded in/affixed to your Ford station wagon to go on one of these "gay and relaxed" outings described above. The book's many color photographs are a picture-window-to-the-past of how station wagons were used as homes-away-from-home and how efficient use of a wagon's cargo space was a priority. One chapter of the book was devoted to "Household Gadgetry for the Car" including coffee makers, shavers, lamps, furniture, and camp tools. Another guides the hunter/fisherman in the family with tips on portable fishing shanties and hunting blinds, heaters, and packsacks.

The book was also a travel guide in that it listed 1,300 campgrounds in 35 states, including maps to locate these havens of peace and serenity. Other areas of interest in the book include: beach and water outings, taking the children along (cribs, car seats, playpens and luminous jackets), and packing and loading techniques for the Ford station wagons that "easily swallow a lot of bulky equipment."

Ephemera, or paper collectibles devoted to station wagons is abundant. The list includes new model dealer postcards, factory photographs, factory sales brochures, owner's manuals and books (including a 1994 fiction paperback book titled *Death By Station Wagon: A Suburban Detective Mystery*, by Jon Katz, in which a wagon has a crucial part in the plot). Other significant books (each out-of-print and difficult to find) focusing on the station wagon include: *The Station Wagon, Its Saga and Development*, by Bruce Briggs; Crestline's *Great American Woodies and Wagons*, by Donald J. Narus; and, *Vintage Station Wagon Shop Service: Representative Applications For All Wood, Combination and Early Metal Bodies*.

A paper collectible that would most logically be expected to contain cover scenes including station wagons, that being the road map, is one of the most difficult to find examples of. It is the rare–almost nonexistent–road map, from any postwar decade when wagons were the preferred mode of vacation travel, that depicts a wagon filled with family members and roof rack buried under luggage. Sedans seem to have been the map publishers' car of choice for cover material.

Station wagons have also been captured in paintings and drawings depicting the old car hobby, and car-related art has become a solid investment as a collectible. Several of these wagon artworks have appeared on the cover of *Old Cars Weekly News & Marketplace* in recent years as well as other hobby publications. Also, while the examples of which are not too numerous, car show posters and programs are another source of station wagon "art."

Other hobby areas that contain station wagon collectibles include: petroliana signs such as battery or lubricant endorsements that include a station wagon as part of the background, pedal cars (Murray produced a Pontiac station wagon pedal car that looks more like a convertible garbage truck while Garton offered a Mercury "woodie" pedal car that is an absolute thing of beauty), and the assorted trinkets that were service station and dealership giveaways such as ashtrays, calendars and playing cards with auto scenes printed on them.

Ephemera

Road maps are a big part of the ephemera portion of automobilia. As a cover art subject, it would seem logical to have scenes of station wagons loaded with families taking vacation trips, but the opposite is true. Finding a map that depicts any kind of station wagon on the cover is tough. One rare example is this 1961 New York sightseeing guide from Esso. That's a 1960 Buick station wagon heading towards the Dwight D. Eisenhower Lock and Tunnel under the St. Lawrence Seaway.

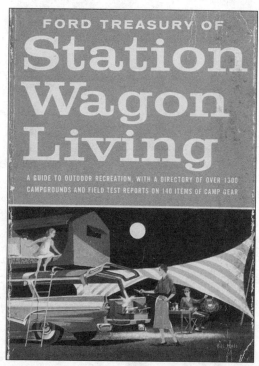

Ford Treasury of Station Wagon Living, published in 1957 by Ford Motor Co., explains how to rig a (Ford) station wagon to take along the comforts of home on a picnic outing or lengthy camping excursion.

208

Another popular collectible in the automotive ephemera niche is sales brochures. Among the many pieces of this type of literature devoted to station wagons are the following:

•1938 Ford

•1960 Ford

•1940 Ford

•1960 Plymouth

•1958 Chevrolet

•1966 Ford

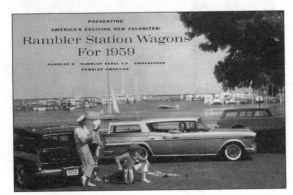

•1959 Rambler

•1982 Chevrolet

Another ephemera collectible in the automobilia hobby is the new model postcard, used to lure potential customers to the dealership. These color postcards usually have a new model staged in some exotic or "outdoorsy" location, and in the case of station wagons often with cargo capacity emphasized via a loaded roof rack or with the car's tailgate open. Among the many station wagon postcards available are the following:

•1955 Chevrolet Two-Ten two-door station wagon

•1961 Dodge Lancer 770 station wagon

•1958 Rambler Super Cross Country station wagon

•1962 Chevrolet Chevy II 300 station wagon

•1960 Studebaker Lark Deluxe two-door station wagon

•1963 Dodge 330 (background) and 440 station wagons

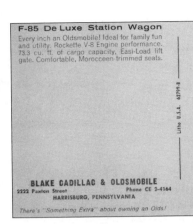

F-85 De Luxe Station Wagon

Every inch an Oldsmobile! Ideal for family fun and utility. Rockette V-8 Engine performance. 73.3 cu. ft. of cargo capacity. Easi-Load lift gate. Comfortable, Morocceen-trimmed seats.

Litho U.S.A. 62799-8

BLAKE CADILLAC & OLDSMOBILE
2222 Paxton Street   Phone CE 2-4164
HARRISBURG, PENNSYLVANIA

There's "Something Extra" about owning an Olds!

•1963 Oldsmobile F-85 Deluxe station wagon (with view of the back of the postcard showing it came from Blake Cdillac-Oldsmobile of Harrisburg, Pennsylvania).

1965 *Mercury* Comet
VILLAGER STATION WAGON

Your car will never again be worth what I can offer you . . . Right Now - - on a New or Used car.

Please ask for Howard J. Shugard

RAHWAY MOTOR CAR CO., INC.
1003 St. George Ave.
Rahway, New Jersey

•1965 Mercury Comet Villager station wagon (with view of the back of the postcard showing it came from Rahway Motor Car Co. of Rahway, New Jersey)

•1965 Pontiac Tempest Custom Safari station wagon

1972 Kingswood Estate Wagon
(Inset) 1927 Chevrolet Capitol Coach

•1972 Chevrolet Kingswood Estate station wagon (with inset of 1927 Chevrolet Capitol coach).

•1968 Pontiac Executive Safari station wagon

•1972 AMC Ambassador Brougham station wagon

Dealer Promotional Models

A 1/20th scale 1953 Chevrolet 150 Handyman station wagon dealer promotional model by Product Miniature Co. (PMC).

A 1/25th scale 1956 Chevrolet Bel Air station wagon dealer promotional model by Product Miniature Co. (PMC).

A 1/25th scale 1957 Chevrolet Bel Air station wagon dealer promotional model by Scale Model Products (SMP).

A 1/25th scale 1959 Ford Country Sedan station wagon dealer promotional model by Product Miniature Co. (PMC).

A 1/25th scale 1960 Chevrolet Nomad station wagon dealer promotional model by Scale Model Products (SMP).

A 1/25th scale 1960 Plymouth Sport Suburban station wagon dealer promotional model by Johan.

A 1/25th scale 1960 Ford Country Sedan station wagon dealer promotional model by Hubley.

A 1/25th scale 1965 Chevrolet Chevelle Malibu station wagon dealer promotional model by AMT Corp.

Model Kits

A 1/25th scale 1931 Ford Model A "woodie" plastic model kit by Revell-Monogram.

A 1/25th scale 1960 Plymouth Suburban Police Emergency Wagon plastic model kit, #C-5100, by Johan.

A 1/25th scale 1965 Chevrolet Chevelle "Super-wagon" drag racing station wagon plastic model kit, #T-411, by AMT Corp.

Toys

Dinky Toys offered this miniature 1948 Plymouth Special Deluxe "woodie" station wagon, #27F.

Tootsietoy offered a miniature 1956 Pontiac Star Chief Custom Safari two-door station wagon (left), #895, as well as a Mercedes-Benz 300SL coupe.

Tootsietoy also offered a miniature 1954 Buick Century Estate Wagon (left) and 1948 Buick Super Estate Wagon (right) as well as a 1949 Buick sedan (center).

Matchbox offered this miniature 1956 Ford "Customline" (Country Sedan) station wagon, #31-A, with gray plastic wheels.

Matchbox also offered this miniature 1963 Studebaker Lark Wagonaire, #42-B, with sliding rear roof panel. This issue also featured a white plastic hunter and either one or two white plastic dogs.

Art

Vol. 26, No. 27, July 17, 1997

Old Cars weekly news & marketplace

WONDERFUL WORLD OF WAGONS

ASHLAND

ASHLAND OIL PRODUCTS

This issue salutes the station wagon. No car-loving kid loved a wagon, but in many cases, that's what our practical parents drove. Wagons led rough lives, and their survival rate is low. This blend of personal experience and rarity tends to make old station wagons popular.
The cover shows Jack Schmitt's painting "Flying Octane." It depicts one of the most popular wagons – the '57 Chevy Nomad – meeting a postwar Ford ragtop at the gas pumps. Inside, you'll find stories about all kinds of wagons.

Automotive works of art have graced the covers of *Old Cars Weekly News & Marketplace* for years. Among these images depicting the best of the old car hobby have been several focusing on the station wagon. One of the most recent has been Jack Schmitt's "Flying Octane" recreation of a 1950s service station meeting of a 1957 Nomad and postwar Ford convertible. This July 17, 1997, issue of *Old Cars Weekly* also had a theme of "Wonderful World of Wagons."

Todd Groesbeck's recreation of the tail-gate view of a 1960 Plymouth Sport Suburban, personalized on its license plate as "60RDHOG," appeared on the *Old Cars Weekly* cover of the March 9, 1995, issue.

Wayne Huffacker's unnamed art also graced the cover of an issue of *Old Cars Weekly* (Feb. 9, 1995), this piece depicting a 1946 Ford "woodie" wagon pulling an early travel trailer, stopped for refueling at a Mobilgas station.

Car show posters and programs are also a source of collectible "artwork" devoted to the station wagon. These two examples are from the Iola Old Car Show, held every July in Iola, Wis. That event's 1988 and 1991 show poster and directory cover featured "woodie" wagons, a 1946 Mercury and 1941 Chrysler Town & Country, respectively.

While beer can graphics are hardly considered "art," the packaging of automotive products such as hard parts as well as commemorative item packaging such as this 1988 Iola Old Car Show "Woodie" tribute beer can fall into the realm of station wagon collectibles.

Station Wagon Innovations

Thriving on competition has always been the cornerstone of the American automobile industry. It involves the simple law of demand and supply: Build cars that become in demand and supply your dealers with just enough of these cars to satisfy that demand. No one manufacturer has been able to dominate the automobile sales landscape for long before a competing maker launched a new product that created consumer demand. This need for makers to continually "build a better mousetrap" to survive has obviously fueled the advance of automobile design. One of the cars that has benefited the most from this better mousetrap mindset has been the station wagon.

The best—and quickest—view of the advance of the station wagon through time is to flip through first the prewar and then the postwar photo gallery sections of this book. The evolutionary stages that are evident include the open-air wood bodies giving way to closed bodies merging steel and wood leading to all-steel bodies with passenger compartments easily converted into cargo space and, finally, transforming into ergonomically designed "chambers" offering creature comforts normally associated with a home.

The number of innovations integrated into station wagons through the years is countless. Some were major breakthroughs, such as the variable-opening tailgate and the Skyroof (Buick's name) treatment for Buick's Sportwagon and Oldsmobile's Vista Cruiser. Others were smaller, yet important gains in functionality, which often went unheralded. All, though, contributed to the evolution of the station wagon.

Most of the innovations that are illustrated as part of this story are not unique to nor did they originate on the car depicted. Design breakthroughs usually originate with one maker, but soon thereafter appear in similar fashion on the cars of competing makers. Considering the "hum" and news stream emanating from the makers' legal departments in Detroit, we can assume these manufacturers do not consider imitation to be the sincerest form of flattery.

A unique approach to generating cargo space involved creating a station wagon-like atmosphere within a sedan, usually called a utility sedan. Several makers including Chrysler, DeSoto and Kaiser-Frazer offered versions of this two-in-one car. This 1949 Kaiser Vagabond (not to be confused with the 1951 Frazer Vagabond) had the upper portion of its hatch—comprised of the rear window and upper trunk lid—covered with a windowed "tent" offered by an aftermarket manufacturer. The rear seat of this sedan could be folded down and the rear compartment of the car offered station wagon-like cargo space, or in this case a place to sleep. The lower trunk lid could be opened via the handle visible and set down for easy loading of cargo. The Kaiser Traveler (pictured in the accompanying full-page ad) was the base sedan while this Kaiser Vagabond featured a leather interior and was the deluxe model.

Maybe you

don't own a pony...

but here's the world's most useful car!

The big, beautiful **Kaiser Traveler**

2-cars-in-one...

only **$2088***

For Farmers; Small Businessmen: Kaiser Traveler is world's only Sunday-go-to-meeting, Monday-go-to-work car. Converts to smart sedan for 6 passengers in 10 seconds. Just fold down back seat, flip open hatch, lower tail-gate. No tools, no bolts.

For Salesmen; Retailers: Big, 10-foot long, steel-shod cargo hold has 130 cubic feet capacity. 123½" wheelbase ends "short car fatigue" on long drives. Powerful Kaiser Thunderhead engine saves gas with 7.3-to-1 high compression ratio.

For Everyone who wants the prestige of owning a big, beautiful, luxurious sedan, but needs a car that can also earn its own way.

Ask your neighborly Kaiser-Frazer dealer for a demonstration

Advertisement for the 1949 Kaiser Traveler four-door sedan, marketed as two-cars-in-one: "Sunday-go-to meeting, Monday-go-to-work." This six-passenger utility sedan offered 130 cubic feet of cargo space.

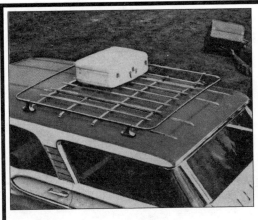

The roof rack/luggage carrier has been a popular piece of station wagon equipment since the early-1940s. Offered both as standard or optional equipment depending on the manufacturer, this application was optional and affixed to a 1958 Mercury Colony Park station wagon.

The second- and third-seat conversion to cargo space has always been a feature of station wagons. In this particular example, a 1960 Ford Country Squire, the cargo load floor was completed after setting down the second and third seats. A variation of this had the second seat, a split-back, only half set down allowing for a "walkway" into the rear compartment.

The variable-opening tailgate was a major breakthrough in station wagon design. The 1966 Ford Country Squire depicted offered the "Magic Doorgate," which opened sideways as a door and dropped down as a tailgate. This Country Squire also offered fold-away dual facing rear seats.

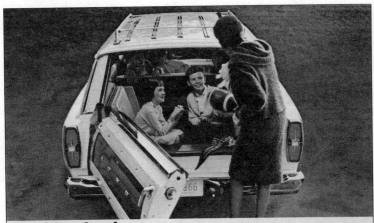

Now it's a door! Ford's exclusive Magic Doorgate is the newest wagon innovation in years. It's a door *and* a tailgate *combined.* Turn the handle and it swings to the side to let people step in more easily and it gives you easier, close-up cargo loading. (Note too Ford's dual-facing rear seats that fold away in a jiffy.)

Now it's a tailgate! When you want an extension of the cargo floor to serve as a platform or picnic table or for long loads (ladders, lumber, rolled carpet), Ford's new Magic Doorgate lowers into place and gives you two more feet of length. It's another great Ford innovation that's standard on *all* '66 Ford wagons.

Pontiac's 1968 line of station wagons was marketed as the "Wide Tracking Wagons" and included the Executive Safari model with optional eight-lug wheels and simulated woodgrain vinyl "planking." Shown is the "Rak Pak" luggage carrier cover that was water- and dust-resistant and could be locked to prevent theft. It also carried a GM logo so it was available for other brands of General Motors station wagons as well.

That same 1968 Pontiac Executive Safari station wagon could also be ordered with an optional utility pad. This coated fabric pad helped keep the cargo area clean and could also be pulled out and used as a ground cushion at picnics or other outdoor events.

Speaking of Safaris and picnics, this optional utility lamp, while not exclusively a station wagon item, was stored under the hood of 1968 Pontiacs. It came with 17 feet of extension cord and was designed as an emergency road light, but came in handy for those evening picnics or card games at the campsite.

The infamous "Wash Me" message printed in the dust by a young ballplayer could be erased by the self-washing electric rear window available on this 1971 Mercury Marquis Colony Park station wagon.

Named differently depending on the manufacturer, Chrysler identified its rear roof "wing" as an airfoil vane. This roof extension accelerated the air over the electrically operated rear window, which prevented dirt from collecting on it when it was up or exhaust fumes from entering the car when it was down.

A close-up view of a "wing," this example from a 1973 Pontiac LeMans Safari station wagon and called a Rear Window Wind Deflector.

Borrowing from a magic act, Pontiac came up with the name "disappearing tailgate" for the power-operated tailgate available on its 1971 Pontiac Safari and Grand Safari station wagons. The window slid up into the roof, while the tailgate slid down under the floor. No "hocus-pocus" was needed as either a key in the tailgate lock or a switch on the instrument panel would activate the tailgate.

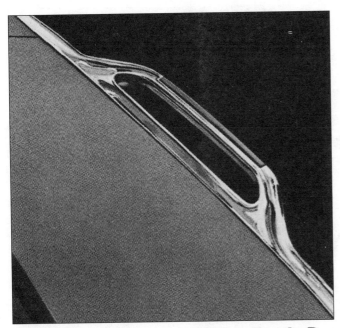

Commonly referred to as assist handles, the D-pillar-attached, optional handles on this 1971 Plymouth Fury Suburban station wagon allowed passengers to enter and exit the rear compartment with ease.

Providing additional interior ventilation on the 1973 Pontiac LeMans Safari station wagon was this rear quarter window vent. It was standard equipment on the three-seat LeMans Safari.

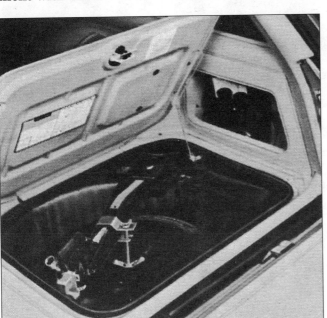

Manufacturers struggled for a long time with placement of the spare tire on (sidemount, tailgate-mounted) and inside their station wagons. With the advent of the "donut" spare tire it allowed makers to place these miniature units in out-of-the-way locations, such as under the cargo floor in this 1983 Oldsmobile Cutlass Cruiser. This Cruiser also provided lockable hidden compartments behind the inner fenderwells for concealing valuables.

Ford offered yet another version of the variable-opening tailgate with the Two-Way Liftgate on its 1984 LTD station wagon. The rear window alone or the entire hatch-type door could be opened, depending on the size of the cargo being placed in the car.

225

Available on select Buick and Oldsmobile station wagons, the elevated Skyroof (Buick's name) was a popular feature that also enhanced the look of the wagons on which it came. This 1969 Olds Vista Cruiser represented the sixth model year the domed, glass paneled roof was offered.

The 1984 Chevrolet Caprice Classic station wagon featured a version of the variable-opening tailgate, this one called the three-way door gate. The window could be lowered to load packages, or the tailgate could be dropped or swung aside for easy access to the third seat.

Rambler slam ads: Belittling the competition=better sales?

In 1960, Rambler's marketing campaign revolved around the theme "X-RAY Checks the 1960 Cars." While relatively tame—at times, comical—by the standards of some modern negative ad campaigns, it was nonetheless an uncommon approach to promoting one brand of automobile as being better than the competition. In factory literature promoting Rambler's line of 1960 station wagons, the campaign was labeled "X-Ray Checks Station Wagons on the Basis of Usefulness to the User." The Rambler wagons were compared in several categories to the wagons of Chevrolet, Ford and Plymouth.

Among the comparison ad copy was Rambler calling the 1960 Chevy wagon "...big, bulky, hard-to-park...." The Ford got off pretty easy, also being touted as "...harder to park." Plymouth caught the brunt of Rambler's "trash talk" being labeled as "unwieldy" and having an "...overgrown fin design...."

The degree to which the "Big Three" makers counter-attacked Rambler in their marketing campaigns is not known. One thing to remember, though. Chevrolet, Ford and Plymouth are still building cars almost 40 years after the X-RAY scrutiny while Rambler is but a distant memory as a manufacturer!

X-RAY

Checks Station Wagons on the

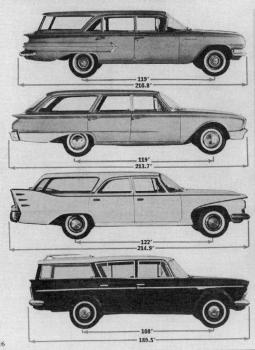

119"
210.8"

119"
213.7"

122"
214.9"

108"
189.5"

47.6"
80.8"

43.0"
81.5"

49.2"
78.6"

50.8"
72.2"

CHEVROLET

The 1960 Chevrolet station wagons retain their unwieldy over-all length and are even wider than before. Yet these big, bulky, hard-to-park wagons offer no more load-carrying capacity than did their counterparts of five years ago.

FORD

The 1960 Ford station wagons have upped their over-all length by more than 5½ inches and their width by approximately the same amount. This increased length and width only makes these cars even harder to park.

PLYMOUTH

Plymouth is the longest of all the standard-sized station wagons — 214.9 inches. But that is only part of its unwieldy size story. For the overgrown fin design makes Plymouth much harder to park, garage and handle in traffic.

RAMBLER

Rambler is the one *compact* station wagon. Its 189.5 inches of over-all length and 72.2 inch width means that Rambler fits any garage with room to spare . . . parks where other's can't . . . offers economy, comfort and performance without bulk.

16

Basis of Usefulness to the User . . .

Ford's upper tail-gate, when left open, rattles and is unsafe for children. This type of "head-cracking, stick-out" tail-gate makes loading difficult.

Rambler's roll-down rear window is safe for children. The one-piece tail-gate can be locked in three positions for the utmost convenience.

It's actually a difficult job to convert the rear seat in the Plymouth station wagon to form the rear deck into a cargo area.

The Rambler rear seat-back can be lowered flush to the floor with fingertip ease to give additional cargo space. No need to move cushion.

Others with 3rd-seat rear entry require passengers to climb over tail-gate, an awkward maneuver. Passengers depend on others to close tail-gate.

Rambler's exclusive 5th-door swings wide, permitting convenient entry and exit. Passengers can close the door. When locked it must be opened with a key.

Ford's slanted rear design in station wagons reduces available cargo room.

Rambler's clean, straight rear styling makes full use of the ample cargo space.

BOX SCORE ON STATION WAGONS

	RAMBLER	Chevrolet	Ford	Plymouth	Dart
Wheelbase	108.0	119.0	119.0	122.0	122.0
Length	189.5	210.8	213.7	214.9	214.8
Width	72.2	80.8	81.5	78.6	78.0
Height	57.3	56.3	56.5	55.4	55.4
Tail-Gate Width at Floor	50.8	47.6	43.0	49.2	49.2
Roof-Top Rack Standard	Yes	No	No	No	No
Roll-Down Tail-Gate Window	Yes	Yes	No	Yes	Yes
Counterbalanced Tail-Gate	Yes	No	No	No	No
5th Door for 3-Seat Models	Yes	No	No	No	No
3rd Seat Facing Direction	Rear	Rear	Front	Rear	Rear
3-Seat Models	6 or V-8	6 or V-8	6 or V-8	V-8 only	6 or V-8
Gas Tank, Gallons	22	17—2 Seat 18—3 Seat	20	22	22
Tire Size	6.40 x 15(1)	8.00 x 14	8.00 x 14	7.50 x 14(2)	8.00 x 14
Horsepower, 6 and V-8 (Standard)	127, 200	135, 170	145, 185	145, 230	145, 230
Curb Weight, Standard Transmission, Middle-Priced, 4-Door, 2-Seat	6:3191 V-8: 3528	6:4090 V-8: 4095	6:4120 V-8: 4221	6:3929 V-8: 4085	6:3999 V-8: 4195
Weight per HP, 6 and V-8 (low best)	25.1, 17.6	30.1, 24.1	28.4, 22.8	27.1, 17.8	27.6, 18.2

(1) 6.70 x 15 Opt. on Six; 7.50 x 14 Std. on V-8.   (2) 8.00 x 14 Std. on 3-Seat Wagon.

17

Pin-Points Station Wagon

FORD

RAMBLER

PLYMOUTH

Try to put a 10-foot long object — like an extension-ladder — in the cargo area of a Ford station wagon. As in other competitive wagons, the ladder will extend out over the tail-gate opening.

The same 10-foot ladder fits entirely within the 1960 Rambler Cross Country. The folded down right front seat gives added cargo space . . . is indicative of Rambler's roominess.

Check the difference in spare tire positions in the station wagon field. The Plymouth and Chevrolet spare tires are carried in inaccessible, inconvenient deep wells. As the pictures show, they are awkward to get at. On the other hand, Rambler's spare tire is easy and convenient to reach, another evidence of Rambler's superior usefulness to the user.

CHEVROLET

RAMBLER

CHEVROLET

RAMBLER

Chevrolet station wagon rear styling dictates a narrow tail-gate opening that seriously detracts from its usefulness to the user.

Rambler's wide, convenient height tail-gate opening provides the maximum width for easy loading and practical usefulness.

18

Features and Advantages

The degree of usefulness of a station wagon to its owner depends upon the features and advantages it offers. X-Ray checks the basic features of the standard-sized station wagons to help you make a valid choice.

CHEVROLET

PLYMOUTH

RAMBLER

It takes real brawn to lift the tail-gates on Chevrolet and Plymouth station wagons. Ladies find them extremely burdensome. Contrast the easy lifting Rambler tail-gate. It can be raised and lowered with scarcely more than fingertip pressure, thanks to counterbalanced design.

RAMBLER FEATURES

Rambler's smart Roof-Top Travel Rack carries extra luggage, camping gear . . . adds to the distinctive Rambler appearance.

A family of 4 or 5 people can sleep in comfort in the Rambler station wagon. Twin Travel Beds, plus large cargo area, make this feature possible.

Even a canoe or rowboat can be stowed with ease in the spacious 80 cubic foot cargo space of the Rambler station wagon, with room to spare.

The tail-gate is a swing-out fifth door in the Rambler 3-seat station wagon. The fifth door can be locked from either inside or outside.

Selling a Station Wagon

**A look at the "Big Three" advertising campaigns
for selling station wagons during the boom years
of wagon sales in the late-1950s/early 1960s.**

Plymouth Wagon—getting in and out of parking spaces is no work at all in No. 1 low-priced economy wagon.

Smoothest-riding wagons on the road. Famous Torsion-Aire suspension gives you a "cloud smooth" ride even on rough roads. Standard equipment on all models.

More room, less noise. Solid welded Unibody ends the major cause of squeaks and rattles, adds inches of space inside.

Chrysler Corporation
Serving America's new quest for quality
PLYMOUTH   VALIANT   •   DODGE   DART   LANCER   •   CHRYSLER   IMPERIAL

Chrysler Wagon—smart looks and luxury in quiet, roomy wagons that fit any setting.

Dodge Dart Wagon—full-size Dodge priced model for model with Ford and Chevrolet.

It's a pretty cool customer
who won't warm up to <u>this</u> wagon!

You have a choice of five handy, handsome Chevy wagons—with the widest seating, widest cargo area and widest selection of engines and transmissions in the low-price field. Whatever the need of the moment—whether it's space for toting a tribe of noisy youngsters to a weekday matinee or for packing picnic paraphernalia on a quiet Sunday afternoon—these Chevrolets are beautifully, dutifully built to do the job. Your dealer's waiting with all the details.

Roomier Body by Fisher *with a lower and narrower transmission tunnel that gives more foot room.*

Pride-pleasing style *(combines good looks with good sense—that handy one-piece tailgate, for instance).*

New Economy Turbo-Fire V8 *(makes friends fast by getting up to 10% more miles on a gallon).*

Shift-free Turboglide*—*only car in its field with automatic drive that eliminates even a hint of a shift.*

Hi-Thrift 6 *(with economy camshaft and carburetion—and Chevy's ever-faithful dependability).*

Coil springs at all 4 wheels *(with the extra cushioning of newly designed body mounts).*

Quicker stopping Safety-Master brakes *(specially designed for long lining wear).*

Chevrolet Division of General Motors, Detroit 2, Michigan

CHEVROLET

*Optional at extra cost.

There's nothing like a new car—and no new car like a '60 Chevrolet. The Kingswood Station Wagon.

230

If you like wagons, you must read this

Rear-facing "Observation Lounge"

One-piece tailgate, power window

Seats fold to form level platform

95 cubic feet of cargo space

You station wagon owners are a sort of special breed. You lead a more active family and social life. You simply *do* more things.

We've built a Dodge wagon that fits into your living pattern like nothing else on wheels.

This Dodge 4-door Sierra is the first wagon to solve the third seat problem with its "Observation Lounge." Passengers board at the rear, face the rear. It's comfortable *and* fun.

The reason you can enter at the rear is because Dodge developed a wonderfully simple *one-piece* tailgate. The window lowers right into it. There's no awkward *upper* liftgate to struggle with or bump your head on when entering or loading.

Now let's convert for hauling. Fold the third seat down and you've got a sizeable rear cargo platform. Want a lot of room? Fold the second seat too, and you've got a flat deck with 95 cubic feet of clear space.

We'd like to send you a descriptive folder on this superb Dodge Sierra wagon. Drop us a card with your name and address: Dodge Station Wagons, Dept. D, Box 1259, Detroit 31, Michigan.

'59 DODGE

Dodge brings you Lawrence Welk on television every week, ABC-TV network. Ask your Dodge dealer for time and channel.

Ford's new 9-passenger Country Squire

Full-size or new-size

Ford gives you the most in wagons!

Senior members of the world's most complete wagon family are the 5 big Ford

wagons... featuring such unique Ford wonders as: the lowest price* in the full-size

field RANCH WAGON ...the biggest cargo space in the field OVER 97 CUBIC FEET ...the most comfort,

convenience and styling elegance in the wagon field... Thunderbird performance too!

Considering a compact? There's nothing to match Ford's two new-size wonders...

the Tudor and Fordor Falcon Wagons... America's lowest priced 6-passenger Wagons*

 FALCONS IN SAVINGS ...with a cargo area longer than any other compact wagon  OVER 7 FEET LONG INSIDE

greatest gas savings in the new-size field... UP TO 30 MI. PER GAL.

New Falcon Wagon, available in 2-door and 4-door models (shown below)

FORD DIVISION, *Ford Motor Company,*

See all seven wagon wonders from **Ford** America's Wagon Specialists

See "FORD STARTIME" in living color Tuesdays on NBC-TV
*Based on manufacturers' suggested retail delivered prices for comparably equipped models

FORD—*The Finest Fords of a Lifetime*   FALCON—*The New-Size Ford*   THUNDERBIRD—*The World's Most Wanted Car*

FIVE BIG REASONS WHY YOUR NEXT STATION WAGON SHOULD BE A *Plymouth*

If you're driving a wagon now, you've already moved ahead into that pleasant realm where motoring is a little more interesting . . . a little more satisfying . . . than it is for the owners of less exciting cars.

But are you paying an undue premium for your fun? Are you getting all that station wagon money can buy at a low, low budget price?

Plymouth has a story for you if you're driving a wagon of any other make. Size, for example: it's the biggest of the low-price 3. And value: you can pay almost twice as much and not get an inch more room . . . an inch bigger car. (You just can't buy a bigger station wagon at *any* price.) There are other interesting advances and features that put Plymouth far ahead now and make it worth more when you trade. Wouldn't it be wise to see what this most exciting of all station wagons has to offer?

Nobody wants to put *enjoyment* solely on a bookkeeping basis, but a good look at the Plymouth wagon . . . a ride in it . . . a study of its low cost and high value . . . is very likely to satisfy you that this time you can own a wagon-load of glamour and save money as well.

1 BIGGEST IN THE LOW-PRICE 3! Longest over-all. 122-inch wheelbase. Cargo deck a foot longer than in "other two." Big as wagons costing thousands more! Ideal for vacation trips.

2 HOLDS MUCH MORE THAN THE "OTHER TWO"! 7 cubic feet more cargo space than wagons C and F, plus extra 7.5-cu.-foot secret luggage compartment in 6-passenger models.

← 17¾ FEET LONG →

3 WIDE-VIEW OBSERVATION SEAT! Easy to enter. Folds flush in floor when not in use. A Plymouth low-price 3 exclusive. You have to lift out 3rd seat of "other two."

4 REAR WINDOW DISAPPEARS! Another Plymouth exclusive in its field! Window rolls into lower section. No clumsy overhanging tailgate for Plymouth owners.

5 AND IT RIDES WITH BIG CAR LUXURY! Floating Torsion-Aire Ride—Plymouth's top-luxury ride at no extra cost! No sway or lurch on turns . . . no nose-dive on stops!

Time Machines With Tailgates

Webster's New World Dictionary has a pretty straight-forward definition of **station wagon:** "*An automobile with more cargo space than a comparable sedan model, two or four doors, a rear seat that folds down, and a rear door hinged in various ways.*"

It might seem, then, that with Detroit's annual push to emphasize "the fresh and new" on the better-selling sedans, hardtops and convertibles that the designers who styled station wagons each year were bound to this cut-and-dried dictionary definition. This, of course, would be apart from what innovative "various way" the tailgate might be hinged.

For the most part, this was probably true. But, as the following photographs show, the station wagon did not totally elude the automobile designers' visions of what a wagon *could* be, given enough leeway. And while most of these concept station wagons never reached production (or were designed knowing that the finished product would end up in the crusher after its brief auto show circuit life span) many of the ideas incorporated into these futuristic vehicles eventually found their way into assembly line station wagons.

From concept station wagons with mild trim and/or accessory upgrades to designs developed to shatter preconceived notions of what a wagon should look like, Detroit tried it all.

Displayed at the 1954 General Motors Motorama was this quartet of pre-production/experimental Corvettes including the Nomad in the center. The two-door station wagon resembled the Corvette and used many components of the production Corvette. However, it was built on a standard Chevrolet chassis and utilized the 150-hp six-cylinder Corvette engine.

Featuring a Western motif, this 1956 Plainsman experimental station wagon was a corporate "idea car" for Chrysler. The Plainsman used a 1955 Plymouth V-8 engine and chassis. The two-door, eight-passenger station wagon offered several innovations that eventually reached production, including a rear-facing third seat and spare tire carried within the right rear fender and accessible by a long panel that enclosed the drive wheel. The roof canopy was vinyl covered. Wheelbase measured 115 inches while overall length was 208 inches. (Photo courtesy of Phil Hall)

The nine-passenger Cabana station wagon joined the car show circuit in 1958. It was built by Ghia of Italy and utilized a Plymouth chassis, but had no engine or transmission. A four-door hardtop by design, the doors were center locked to floor-height pillars, which provided maximum side access. The unique "tailgate" was a full-width, side-opening, power-hinged door. Two sliding clear plastic roof panels aided rear seat entry as well as adding to usable cargo height. The Cabana's steel roof had a skylight at the front. All except the driver's seat could be folded down to maximize carpeted cargo space. Wheelbase measured 124 inches while overall length was 215.8 inches.

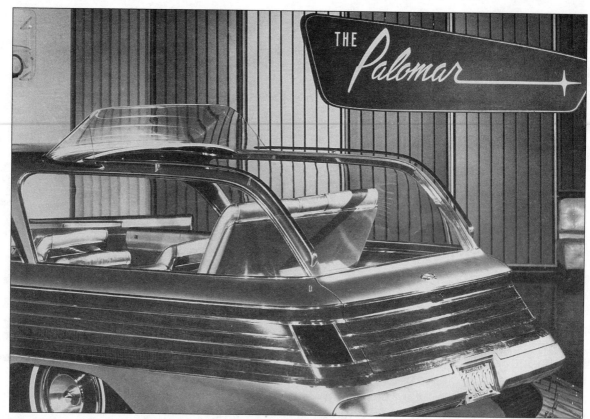

Mt. Palomar had one of the largest reflecting telescopes for looking into space and was the inspiration for the 1962 Ford Palomar. The Palomar featured a powerboat-like "flying bridge" for rear passengers. The rear part of the roof folded away into the front section, similar to how a roll-top desk operates. The third seat was elevated and those passengers were protected by a second windshield mounted in the middle of the roof.

As the modern license plate reads, this "One Off" station wagon was an American Motors styling exercise based on the 1962 Ambassador Cross Country. Named the "Vegas," it toured on the 1962 auto show circuit. The Vegas was powered by a 327-cid V-8 engine.

Displayed in the Ford Pavilion at the 1964 New York World's Fair was this Aurora concept station wagon. Based on a 131-inch wheelbase Mercury chassis, the Aurora measured 227.55 inches overall. Replacing the conventional grille was a bank of 12 one-inch sealed beam headlamps. The Aurora featured a built-in roll bar, and an electric release automatically locked all doors when the transmission was

shifted into any drive position. For comfort, the interior offered contoured seats, and the front passenger swivel seat could be turned to face the J-shaped lounge so front and rear passengers could face each other. In addition to air conditioning, the interior featured an AM-FM radio, plug-in television set, thermoelectric oven and refrigerator, and a bar and cabinet for storing ice, beverages and glasses. In addition to the radio and television, the communications console encompassed a card recorder that Ford stylists envisioned for use in playing pre-recorded music, feeding pre-recorded movies to the television's viewing screen or dictating letters. The driver of the Aurora steered with an unconventional airplane-like steering bar with side grips. Power-assisted, variable-ratio steering re-

quired only one-half turn lock-to-lock. Automatic speed control was offered, and, for turnpike driving, there was a panel that automatically informed the safe speed for any lane and flashed signals of changing turnpike information. An illuminated instrument panel road map could be manually operated or preset to roll with the progress of the car. The windshield of the Aurora extended into the roof area where it met the polarizing sun roof. By the touch of a button, the driver could control the amount of sunlight through the sun roof – from opaque to transparent to varying shades of soft green.

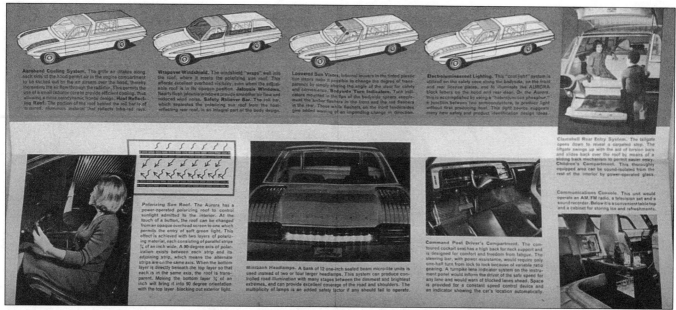

At the rear of the Aurora, Ford designed in what it called a "romper room" area separated from the main cabin by a vertical power-operated window. This "room" featured a coved, rear-facing seat, storage space along the sides for books and toys, separate temperature control button, and separate AM/FM radio that doubled as an intercom. The area was accessed via a "clam-shell" rear entrance that offered a carpeted step on the counter-balanced tailgate. Also, the back of the rear-facing seat folded down to provide access to the luggage area between compartments.

The 1968 AMX III concept station wagon featured hardtop styling reminiscent of the 1956 Rambler wagons. Painted a silver metallic, the AMX III's unique tailgate lifted up and through the use of scissor-action hinges slid forward to rest on the roof. (Photo courtesy of Phil Hall)

Ford Division unveiled the "Magic-Cruiser" concept version of its Galaxie 500 at the 1966 Chicago Auto Show. A fastback design (top), the Magic-Cruiser could be quickly transformed into a station wagon (below) when the fastback section of the car's roof and two special window side panels were electrically raised. Lowering of the tailgate permitted easy entry to a rear-facing third seat. Folding down the second and third seats provided a carpeted cargo bed. (Photo courtesy of Phil Hall)

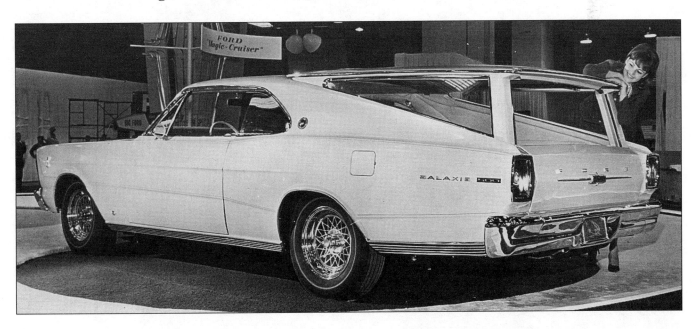

Another generation of the Aurora, the Aurora II was a concept station wagon derived from Ford's 1969 LTD Country Squire. The Aurora II featured a luxury lounge area of soft, curved seats and a swivel front passenger seat. Passenger side doors swung out for easy entrance and exit. The rear tailgate gave access to a second lounge area complete with Philco-Ford television set. (Photo courtesy of Phil Hall)

Even the Chevrolet Camaro was fitted with kammback
styling in the early 1970s to try to make this pony car
more "family-oriented" or at least more cargo-friendly.

Not to be left out of General Motors' pony car-to-station wagon experiments was the Pontiac Trans Am, this version created in 1978 and named the Type K. Instead of a formal tailgate, side-opening glass panels allowed easy access to the cargo compartment. (Photo courtesy of Phil Hall)

Expression*ism*

Visitors to the 1990 Chicago Auto Show had the opportunity to see what was then Oldsmobile's vision of "The New Generation" of family transportation. Called the Expression, this concept car was labeled as a family sport sedan rather than a station wagon.

Displayed on a turntable at the show, from any angle the driveable Expression concept car featured an esthetically pleasing elliptical shape.

Included in Expression's safety features were traction control, four-wheel steering, on-board navigation system, supplemental inflatable restraint system and rain-sensing windshield wipers.

As well as being safe, the Expression had a fun side. It featured a full entertainment center as part of its unique tailgate and backlight assembly and featured a Nintendo game center, VCR, hot and cold storage space and a built-in vacuum cleaner with outlets throughout the car.

Exterior Design

The original sketch of the Expression was done by Tom Peloquin of General Motors' Advanced 3 studio. The car displayed at Chicago did not deviate too much from Peloquin's original drawings.

Expression's low, smooth front fascia continued almost without notice into a flush-mounted windshield and roofline. In fact, all of Expression's fiberglass exterior panels were flush-mounted for a clean appearance.

From the roofline, Expression flowed elliptically to a larger rear end featuring an innovative tailgate and steeply-raked backlight assembly. The rear wrapped around the side panels for a smooth and rounded look and continued the elliptical theme. Expression was finished in flaming red paint with a hint of orange.

Up front, five small headlamps on each side framed the futuristic but recognizable Oldsmobile front fascia. The lamps not only made for an esthetically pleasing front appearance allowing designers to lower the entire front profile, but also provided bright, even lighting of the road surface.

Expression's wheels played an integral part in the overall exterior styling scheme. The 17-inch front and 18-inch rear turbine-like wheels were designed to highlight Expression's low front appearance and higher rear backlight assembly.

Powertrain and Suspension

Powering the Expression was a Quad 4 (2.3-liter, 230-hp) 16-valve four-cylinder engine. It transmitted power to the Expression's front wheels through a four-speed electronically controlled automatic transmission. The flip of a switch electronically moved the transmission from park to reverse or drive.

The front and rear suspension components were basically modified versions of many of GM's proven suspension systems. Expression's traction control system automatically adjusted the power to the front drive wheels.

Expression also featured four-wheel steering – handy in tight parking situations and an instrumental safety feature during evasive maneuvers. In addition, the family sport sedan offered speed sensitive variable effort steering that automatically made steering effort lighter and easier.

For added security, Expression featured four-wheel disc brakes with an anti-lock feature that avoided brake lock-up and allowed directional stability and steering control to be retained during most braking situations.

Interior Design

Expression had a colorful sable and tan all-leather interior with orange piping to match the exterior color. Olds designers opted for a simple, useful interior. Analog gauges and pod-mounted controls graced the instrument panel.

A clean fiberglass strip with contrasting color stripe made its way through Expression's interior in an elliptical shape just below the windows and contained all controls for doors and windows.

Up front, Expression featured a hands-off cellular telephone for added safety and a console-mounted CRT screen with a Navicar navigational system. Expression also featured steering wheel touch controls for the sound and ventilation systems, driver and passenger supplemental inflatable restraints (air bags) and a Head Up Display of primary instruments.

Expression's radio and integral CD player featured separate controls and headsets for each passenger to allow programming of the music of choice. Also, Expression's heating and ventilation system featured a shut-off and direction control for second- and third-seat passengers, assuring comfort for all.

Special attention was also given to interior lighting. Expression featured reading lamps for each seating position as well as indirect lighting that diffused the cabin for a more dramatic appearance.

Expression also offered plenty of storage room with front seat map pockets, door storage pockets and net storage on the back of each seat. A cup holder was also provided to each passenger.

As innovative as Expression was with its safety and convenience features, the tailgate entertainment center was where kids of all ages would find the most fun.

With the flip of a switch the backlight retracted automatically over the roof panel, the tailgate popped open and the entire rear end became an entertainment center complete with video games, a VCR, hot and cold storage cooler and an integral vacuum cleaner with outlets throughout the car.

Many of the safety and convenience features displayed in the Expression have since made their way into production vehicles. As for the Expression, the market for station wagons – even if called a family sport sedan – has been diminished by the minivan craze. Since its days as a show car, the Expression has been stored at Oldsmobile's Plant 4 in Lansing, Mich. There are currently no plans for the car, but Oldsmobile representatives said it will someday be displayed in the nearby R.E.O. Museum.

Expression Technical Specifications

Exterior Dimensions (inches)

Wheelbase	104.9
Overall length	200.3
Overall width	74.4
Overall height	55.0

Interior Dimensions (inches)

Head room front - 38.5 middle - 39.0 rear - 36.5
Shoulder room front - 57.2 middle - 57.2 rear - N/A
Leg room front - 42.1 middle - 35.6 rear - 29.0

Powertrain

Engine - supercharged 2.3-liter DOHC Quad 4
Horsepower - 230
Transmission - four-speed electronic automatic

Suspension

Front - MacPherson strut
Rear - fully independent
four-wheel steering
speed sensitive variable effort steering
four-wheel antilock disc brakes

Other Features

Flat screen color CRT screen with:
•hands-free cellular telephone
•navigation system
•climate control functions
•service reminders
•radio controls
•personal reminder functions

Head Up Display of major instruments
Rain sensing windshield wipers
Auxiliary inflator with outlet hose
Integrated hot/cold storage box
Integrated vacuum cleaner

Third seat entertainment center featuring:
•integral CD player
•video game
•video cassette recorder
•television

Forming an Expression

Craftsmen construct the fiberglass exterior panels of the Oldsmobile Expression family sport sedan.

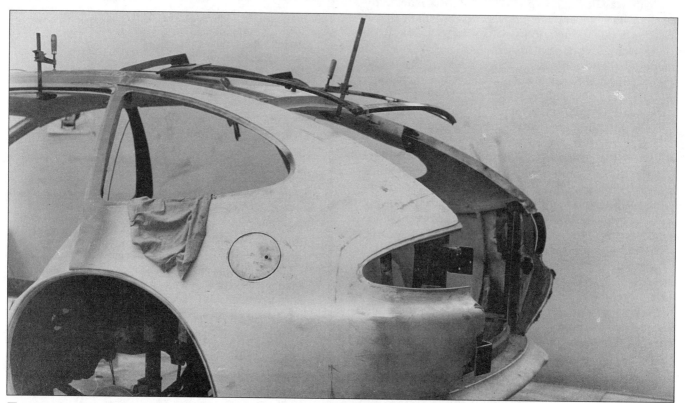

Expression's unique tailgate assembly shows the steel frame that holds the retractable glass rear window.

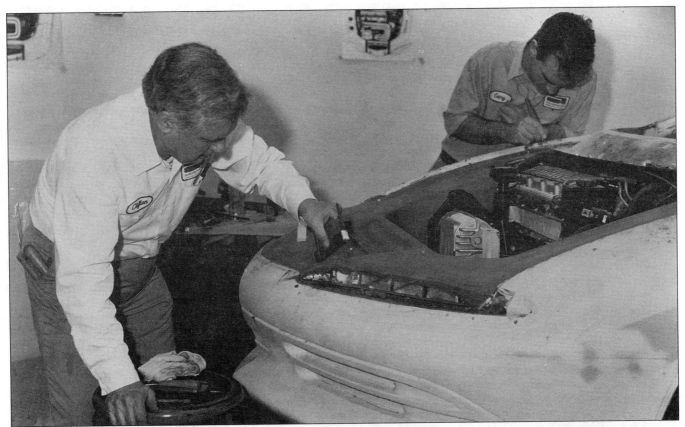

Craftsmen apply the finishing touches under the hood. Even Expression's engine compartment carried the theme of smooth uninterrupted lines and simplicity.

Early view of Expression's body work shows the wind-cheating elliptical shape.

The Expression's unique tailgate assembly doubled as an entertainment center. This close-up shows early work on the tailgate and where the television and video game would be installed.

Overhead view shows the nearly completed body of Expression awaiting the chassis and supercharged 2.3-liter Quad 4 engine.

Close-up view of the completed body shows Expression's smooth front fascia and elliptical shape.

The completed Expression on display at the 1990 Chicago Auto Show.

Draggin' Wagons

by Phil Hall

Station wagons have been around racetracks as long as there have been station wagons. Their initial use was related to their hauling capacity rather than their performance potential for competition.

However, during the 1950s, wagons began to be used in the stock and altered classes in drag racing. While popularity never hit big numbers, a steady parade of draggin' wagons on the nation's dragstrips continues right up to the bracket racing of today.

Wagon bodies also found use from time to time in modified stock car races and on more exotic drag machinery such as funny cars and match racers.

What sets a station wagon apart from a sedan and the reason for it being chosen for selected forms of automotive competition, is what is behind the rear seat. Instead of a trunk is an extended roof over a cargo or third seat area, a heavy tailgate and usually a heavier and reinforced chassis to carry all the stuff the owner cares to fill the inside with.

In race cars, being lighter and smaller is usually an advantage, but not in all cases. Drag racing factors weight against horsepower and has many classes for vehicles high weight and/or low power, so everyone has a chance. While the top power/low weight classes get the most attention, the lower classes, especially for the stocks, allow the little guy to have fun, too.

If you are racing a stock car, the rules make no allowances for body styles. You can run a stripper coupe, fancy convertible or a big old station wagon. While the latter was automatically shunned by the cool guys who dragged their coupes, hardtops and convertibles in the 1950s, the thinking guys looked at the wagons.

Why?

The rear structure put more weight percentage on the rear wheels, and much of it behind them. Since all the stocks were rear wheel drive then, all the weight you could shift off the front and onto the rear was an advantage. Roger Huntington, writing in *Popular Hot Rodding*, estimated as much as 55 percent of the weight could be on the rear wheels with a properly set up station wagon. This compared to around 45 percent for some sedans.

You still had your choice of all the performance engines offered in any given year, so working with numbers, you could pick the class your setup was close to the lowest pounds per advertised horsepower allowed.

Of course rules changed from year to year and stock classes were sub-divided several times over the years in the 1950s through the 1970s, before bracket racing gained the popularity it has today.

Though isolated stock station wagons likely appeared before them, among the early wagons to be noticed by the drag racing set were the 1955-'57 Chevrolets. A wide selection of the new V-8 engines, a nice engine setback in the chassis, solid frame and rap-

idly growing performance parts list helped them in stock and lower gas (modified) competition.

At the 1959 National Hot Rod Association (NHRA) Nationals at Detroit, Jack Feudner set top time in D/Gas with a 1955 Nomad (with a 1957 Chevy engine), besting a field of sedans and hardtops.

However, literally all of the 1955-'57 station wagons were competitive. Witness the runs at the 1964 NHRA show at Detroit by John Cordia in his 1956 nine-passenger wagon, complete with the third seat up and in place. That gave his 265-cid V-8 more rear weight and helped him take the little stock eliminator title.

When rules changed around 1972 to allow older models in the super stock NHRA classes, which permitted 10-inch rear tires (as opposed to seven in the stock classes) and more liberal engine modifications, the 1955-'57 Chevy wagons made the move nicely. Paul Smith's 1955 was the SS Eliminator at the 1973 Winternationals at Pomona, Calif., to start out 1973. It was not unusual.

The International Hot Rod Association (IHRA) Formula Stock winner at Bristol, Tenn., in 1973 was a wheel-standing 1957 Chevy wagon wheeled by Lyle Epperson.

Somewhat paralleling the 1955-'57 Chevy wagon success in the lower stock classes is the somewhat parallel Chevy sedan deliveries of the same vintage. One might ask why a sedan delivery would be used, when a station wagon had more rear weight (and were a whole lot easier to find). The answer was automatic. NHRA classified the sedan deliveries as trucks, which they were. Since Chevy trucks offered the four-speed Hydramatic automatic transmissions as options, NHRA allowed them in sedan deliveries. The Hydramatic was a far superior unit for dragging compared to the two-speed Powerglide the wagons (and the rest of the passenger car line) were saddled with.

Current Petersen Publishing Co. executive John Dianna ran his 1956 sedan delivery in L/Stock Automatic in 1969 and claimed stock eliminator honors three-quarters of the time, all with a 265-cid V-8. He had plenty of company in the panel models.

As popular as the 1955-'57 Chevrolets are and were, nostalgia value doesn't count for anything when you are going through the traps. As bigger engines became available and newer models more plentiful, the popularity of the older Chevy station wagons began to wane in the 1970s. Among those successfully used on dragstrips were the larger full-sized wagons, compact 1962-'67 Chevy IIs and intermediate 1965 and up Chevelles.

Chevrolet gave racers a double whammy for 1958 with a new and controversial X-frame and coil springs all around (as opposed to the ladder frame and rear leaf springs on the older models) and added its exit from factory support at the same time. Acceptance was slow in all forms of stock racing and especially so for the wag-